PENGUIN BOOKS

# LANDSCAPES OF THE
# METROPOLIS OF DEATH

'Otto Dov Kulka has performed a minor miracle. He has written a masterpiece . . . lyrical, incantatory . . . bears witness to the worst that man can do to man, and in doing so testifies to the enduring power of the human spirit' *The Times Literary Supplement*

'Quite simply, extraordinary . . . something strange and powerful formed from, but separate to, the solution of history . . . I can't see how this book could be bettered' *The Times Higher Education*

'This is not history, it is something else . . . his words enter the wider sphere of literature' *Sunday Times*

'Stunning . . . the profound vision of a moral philosopher . . . ironic, probing, present in the past, able to connect the particular with the cosmic' *Guardian*

'The book is not a memoir in the conventional sense, but an extraordinary collection of some of the memories, ideas and dreams that make up Kulka's internal landscape' *Daily Telegraph*

'In this short, powerful memoir, every word tells its story' *Daily Mail*

'Powerful and haunting' *Bloomberg*

## ABOUT THE AUTHOR

Otto Dov Kulka was born in Czechoslovakia in 1933. He is Professor Emeritus at the Hebrew University of Jerusalem.

# OTTO DOV KULKA

# Landscapes of the
# Metropolis of Death

*Reflections on Memory and Imagination*

*Translated by* RALPH MANDEL

PENGUIN BOOKS

PENGUIN BOOKS

UK | USA | Canada | Ireland | Australia
India | New Zealand | South Africa

Penguin Books is part of the Penguin Random House group of companies
whose addresses can be found at global.penguinrandomhouse.com

Penguin
Random House
UK

First published by Allen Lane 2013
Published in Penguin Books 2014
Reissued 2020
001

Text originally written in Hebrew and translated by Ralph Mandel, except
'Ghetto in an Annihilation Camp', which was first presented in English at the Fourth
Yad Vashem International History Conference, January 1980, translated from
Hebrew by Ina Friedman and first published in *The Nazi Concentration Camps*,
edited by Yisrael Gutman and Avital Saf (Jerusalem, 1984; also published in the
same year in Hebrew, by Yad Vashem Publishers, Jerusalem). The text is
republished with permission of Yad Vashem.

'A Prologue that Could Also Be an Epilogue', the section of chapter 2 called
' "Ode to Joy" ', chapter 9 (under the title 'Landscapes of a Private Mythology and the
"Gate of the Law" ') and chapter 10 (under the title 'In Search of History and Memory')
first published in English in *On Germans and Jews under the Nazi Regime: Essays by
Three Generations of Historians: A Festschrift in Honor of Otto Dov Kulka*, edited
by Moshe Zimmermann (The Hebrew University Magnes Press, Jerusalem, 2006).

Typeset by Jouve (UK), Milton Keynes
Printed and bound in Great Britain by Clays Ltd, Elcograf S.p.A.

A CIP catalogue record for this book is available from the British Library

ISBN: 978-0-718-19702-5

www.greenpenguin.co.uk

*There remained the inexplicable landscape of ruins. – History tries to explain the inexplicable. As it comes out of a truth-ground it must in turn end in the inexplicable.*

after a parable by Kafka

## Note to the 2020 Reissue

The response to my book *Landscapes of the Metropolis of Death*, which I decided to publish, after many years of hesitation, in 2013, prompted me to compile documentation about its origins and reception and to make it accessible as an unpublished manuscript in my scholarly and literary estate deposited in the National Library of Israel (Call number ARC.4*2024), under the title

### On the Landscapes of the Metropolis of Death
### Genesis and Reception

Now, seven years after the book's original publication, I welcome the decision of Penguin Books to reissue *Landscapes of the Metropolis of Death*.

Jerusalem, January 2020

# Contents

## Landscapes of the Metropolis of Death

## Three Chapters from the Diaries

CONTENTS

# Acknowledgements

I wish to thank all those whose initiative, skill and willingness to engage me in an ongoing dialogue made this book possible in its present form, first of all Chaia Bekefi, who persuaded me to start recording my reflections. No less meaningful for me were the comments and reactions of readers of the previously published excerpts in English and German, some of whom also read the whole manuscript in its Hebrew original or in the excellent English translation by Ralph Mandel. I greatly enjoyed working with him. Much appreciation is also due to the two translators of the previously published sections of the German version, Anne Birkenhauer and Noa Mkayton, to Gerald Turner, the translator of the three poems by an unknown poet from Auschwitz, as well as to the translator of my article reprinted in the appendix to this book, Ina Friedman.

I owe special thanks to my Israeli-American colleague Saul Friedländer, who was the first to listen to the initial tape-recordings and encouraged me to publish them, though at the time I did not wish to mix my scientific publications with what I call my '*Ausserwissenschaftliches*' (extra-scientific-writings). I am equally grateful to the German literary historian Heinz Brüggemann, who initiated the publishing of the German excerpts and provided them with an extensive introduction, based in part on texts from our exchange of letters on Walter Benjamin, Franz Kafka and W. G. Sebald, and of course on excerpts from the manuscript of this book.

I am deeply indebted to my British colleague Sir Ian Kershaw for our continuous dialogue on historical research, in the course of which he also read and commented on my 'extra-scientific' texts in the various stages of their English translation, as well as to my Israeli, Israeli-American and German colleagues and friends Katarina Bader, Omer Bartov, Menahem Ben-Sasson, Susanne Heim, Dan Laor, Noa Mkayton, Dimitry Shumsky and Susanne Urban.

I also would like to express my great appreciation for the devoted work of the musicologist Moshe Shedletzki, who transformed my rather amateurish tape-recordings into digitized CDs, and assisted me in the selection of the present texts. My special thanks also go to Ada Pagis for permission to include three poems by her late husband Dan Pagis in my present book.

Finally, I wish to thank Yad Vashem, Jerusalem for permission to reprint my article 'Ghetto in the Annihilation Camp' in the appendix to this book, as well as all the archives, libraries, publishers and private owners cited in the List of Illustrations for generously permitting the reproductions of pictures and documents which are integrated in the text.

My warmest thanks and admiration to the splendid editors at Penguin, especially to the publishing director Simon Winder. I very much enjoyed working with him. It was he and his excellent editorial staff Richard Duguid and Marina Kemp, as well as the foreign rights team Kate Burton, Sarah Hunt Cooke and Catherine Wood, who opened the horizon for almost simultaneous editions of the book in many other European languages and worldwide.

# Introduction

I assume that readers of my historical publications will have identified me unequivocally with an attitude of strict and impersonally remote research, always conducted within well-defined historical categories, as a kind of self-contained method unto itself. But few are aware of the existence within me of a dimension of silence, of a choice I made to sever the biographical from the historical past. And fewer still will know that for a decade (between 1991 and 2001) I made tape-recordings which allowed me to describe the images that well up in my memory and explore the remembrance of what in my private mythology is called 'The Metropolis of Death', or in deceptive simplicity: 'Childhood Landscapes of Auschwitz'. These recordings were neither historical testimony nor autobiographical memoir, but the reflections of a person then in his late fifties and sixties, turning over in his mind those fragments of memory and imagination that have remained from the world of the wondering child of ten to eleven that I had once been.

For many years I refrained from publishing the tape recordings. It was only after completing the major research and documentary projects to which I was committed[1] that I decided to make my 'Landscapes' available to the public.

I am aware that, beyond the dichotomy that looms between my scholarly work and my reflective memory, this present book in itself reveals immanent tensions: a confrontation between images of memory and the representation of historical research.

The historical scene was a site called the 'family camp' (*Familienlager*) for the Jews from Theresienstadt at Auschwitz-Birkenau, mainly in the children's and youth block that existed there for nearly a year, until the final liquidation of the camp and almost all its inmates in the summer of 1944.[2]

This book consists of ten chapters taken from these recordings, followed by three chapters of excerpts from my diaries, all from recent years. In their nature and themes these excerpts closely resemble the tape-recorded reflections. Where necessary, I have provided references, mainly for the sources of the quotations and names of persons. Similar to the language of the diaries, the tape-recordings are monologues. The difference is that they were spoken in the presence of the dialogue partner who initiated the recordings and made them possible. In transforming the original spoken word into a printed text I have tried to retain its authentic nature: the immediacy and the rhythm of the spoken word with all its irregularities and distinctive inflections and tonalities.

The visual component integrated into the text constitutes part of the narrative itself. The images are in part my own photographs of the sites I walked through in the narrative as well as photographs, drawings and facsimiles from other sources.

The hidden meaning of the metaphoric language of the central, recurrent motifs in the book, such as 'immutable law of death', the 'Great Death', the 'Metropolis of Death', reaches beyond the experience of the world of Auschwitz. They are metaphors for what at the time seemed to expand into a world order that would change the course of human history and remained so in my reflective memory. I am also aware that these texts, though anchored in concrete historical events, transcend the sphere of history.

# Landscapes of the
# Metropolis of Death

# I

# A Prologue that Could Also Be an Epilogue

The start of this journey – I don't know where it will lead me – is utterly prosaic, strictly routine: an international scientific conference in Poland, in 1978, at which I was one of several Israeli participants. It was held under the auspices of the International Committee of Historical Sciences, specifically the section on comparative history of religion. Our group consisted of one medievalist, one early modern history specialist, and, from the modern era, me, together with another historian to whom the Poles refused entry because he was a former Polish citizen and by immigrating to Israel had 'betrayed the homeland'. The conference went pretty much as conferences go. True, my lecture was quite innovative and generated considerable interest,[1] but that passed. Afterwards the conference hosts organized trips to the far corners of the country – to Kraków, to Lublin and to the beautiful places that are intended for tourists. I told my colleagues that I would not be going with them but would follow a route of my own and go to visit Auschwitz. Well, a Jew going to visit Auschwitz – there's nothing unusual in that, though at the time it wasn't the fashion it is today.

One of my colleagues, the medievalist, whom I had known for quite a few years from the field of our academic work, told me, 'You know, when you go to Auschwitz, don't stay in the main camp, which is a kind of museum. If you're going already, go to Birkenau – that is the real Auschwitz.' He didn't ask if I had any connection with that place. If he had asked, I would have replied. I would not have denied it. But he didn't ask, I didn't reply and I went.

# On the Road up along
# the River of Time

I wanted to take a train but there were no tickets available. So I took a plane to Kraków. In Kraków I got a taxi, a faded antique, and asked the driver to take me to Auschwitz. It wasn't his first trip to that place; he had already taken foreign tourists there. I spoke Polish, and not even such a broken Polish, made up in part from what I knew from then and in part what I had learned at the university, and my foundation in Czech helped, too. We drove along, the chatterbox of a driver chattering about his car having been stolen and returned to him, driving along the River Vistula (Wisła) while he told me about 'Wisła zła', meaning the 'wicked Vistula', which overflows and floods the countryside, sweeping away people and cattle. We travelled along roads that were more or less tarmacked, over potholes, and gradually I stopped replying. I stopped taking in what he was saying. I took in that road. I suddenly had the feeling of having already been in these places. I knew the signs, these houses. True, it was a different landscape, a wintry night landscape – especially that first night, though also a landscape of days – and I understood something I hadn't planned for: that I was travelling in the opposite direction on the road that led me, on 18 January 1945, and on the days that followed, out of that complex about which I was certain, about which we were all certain, that it was a complex no one ever came out of.

# The Night Journey of
# 18 January 1945

That journey has many faces, but it has one face, perhaps one colour, one night colour, which was preserved with an intensity that exceeds all the others, one that is identified – that intensity or that night colour – with that journey, which was afterwards called the 'death march'. It was a journey to freedom; it was a journey through those gates out of which no one ever thought we would pass.

What I remember from that journey – in fact, I remember everything, but what is dominant – is, as I said, a certain colour: a night colour of snow all around, of a very long convoy, black, moving slowly, and suddenly – black stains along the sides of the road: a large black stain and then another large black stain, and another stain ...

I.

At first I was intoxicated by the whiteness, by the freedom, by having left behind the barbed-wire fences, by that wide-open night landscape, by the villages we passed. Then I looked more closely at one of the dark stains, and another – and I saw what they were: human bodies. The stains multiplied, the population of corpses increased.

I was exposed to this phenomenon because as the journey dragged on my strength increasingly waned, and I found myself ever closer to the last rows, and in those last rows anyone who faltered, anyone who lagged behind, was shot and became a black stain by the road-side. The shots grew more frequent and the stains proliferated until, miraculously, totally unexpectedly – at least for us – the convoy stopped on the first morning.

I am not going to describe this death march now, or the escape and all the rest. I have described here only one association that arose from the chatter of the driver from Kraków, from the River Vistula which overflowed, which wound its way along all those roads that drew closer and closer to places I recognized. I recognized them in some sort of dream way. Maybe I didn't recognize them and only imagined that I did, but that is of no significance. I fell silent and finally asked him to be silent, too.

We arrived there and I asked him if he knew the way, not to the museums – not to Auschwitz I – but to Birkenau.

## The Red Brick Gate of the Metropolis. The Landscapes of Silence and Desolation from Horizon to Horizon. The Burial of Auschwitz

We arrived at that gate, the red-brick gate with the tower, beneath which the trains passed. I knew it so well. I asked him to wait by the side outside the gate. I didn't want him to go in there. It was a rainy summer day, not pouring, but an annoying drizzle that hovered relentlessly and saturated the air with a mix of fog and a damp, silent visibility – as much as an annoying drizzle like that can be silent.

After he parked the car I walked along the track, between the tracks, where grass now grew, through that gate, for the second time – but that day on foot, under my own steam. I went to a place where I was sure of my way. It was one of the camps that should have been there, but in place of the camp, stretching from horizon to horizon, were rows – forests – of brick chimneys that were left from the barracks that had been dismantled and had disappeared, and tottering concrete pillars, each leaning in a different direction, and rusting shreds of barbed wire on this side and on that side – some lay still, others crept in the damp grass – the damp wet grass – from horizon to horizon.

And the silence. An overwhelming silence. Not even the sound of a bird was heard there. There was muteness there, and emptiness there. There was astonishment that these landscapes – which had been so densely crowded with people, like ants, with armies of slaves, with

2.

rows of people making their way along the paths – were silent. Were deserted. But everything was there: there was that forest of concrete pillars – one could almost see them proud and erect, with those taut steel wires, as on the day we entered, at night – as in that night illuminated with a pageant of lights passing over our faces at the slow entry of the train to that 'corridor of lights, to the Metropolis of Death'.

But it was no longer the Metropolis of Death that it had been. It was a very melancholy landscape. A landscape fraught with desolation. But everything was there, though at a kind of distance. At a distance of desolation, but very searing. As searing as on that day – no, it wasn't so innocent. It was no longer a childhood landscape, it was a landscape of – I don't want to say this word – but it was a graveyard landscape, the burial of Auschwitz. Auschwitz had been buried. Buried but nonetheless expansive, like a kind of vast grave from horizon to horizon. But everything was there, and I, at least, was able to recognize it.

3.

## On the Ruins of the 'Youth and Children's Block' and the 'Hospital Block'

The first place I went to across that grass was the foundations of the youth and children's block, the cultural centre of that unique camp, about which I will speak elsewhere. I picked up one mouldy brick – a fragment of a brick – and took it with me.

I went according to the numbering there. I identified the place according to the rows of barracks whose foundations stood in a row, and I knew that this was block thirty-one. From there I went to the compound of another place, where the hospital block had stood, the block in which the notorious Doctor Mengele carried out his experiments, in which I had been a patient for a certain period, ill with diphtheria, and, paradoxically, that very illness which then seemed fatal saved my life. There, too, I first absorbed a considerable portion of European cultural heritage, transmitted by a dying inmate. To the boy that he believed would ... might come out of there. And he really did come out of there, and took that with him. (But about that, too, I will talk in another chapter.)

So much for the trip to two places in which I had really been, two buildings that I entered back then, in which I lived back then, in which I absorbed what I absorbed, which has remained with me.

## The Way to the Place of the Third Destruction – 'Prometheus in Hades'

From here, the way to the third place was unavoidable, the place where I seemingly lived and remained always, from that day to this, and I am held captive there as a life prisoner, bound and fettered with chains that cannot be undone. Were it not so grating, I would say, 'like Prometheus bound'. But I am after all a child, who was bound with those chains as a child and remained bound by them throughout every stage of growing up.

I say that I was bound and remained bound, or fettered by chains, but that is because I was never there, because my foot never stepped into those courtyards, inside those buildings. I circled them as a moth circles a flame, knowing that falling into it was inevitable, yet I kept on circling outside, willingly or unwillingly – it was not up to me – all my friends, the butterflies, not all of them, but almost all of them, were there and did not come out of there.

## The Circles of Return to (and from) the Metropolis of Death

The place I went to was of course the place of the crematoria. The first one I arrived at was No. II, I think. It was blown up by the Nazis, as was No. I, opposite, and both have been partly preserved. There were bushes and trees there, growing wild on those ruins. From there I took a fragment of a second brick, black and sooty. Then I went

4.

across the way to Crematorium No. I, the underground gas chamber of which was not destroyed when it was blown up. The stairs that led to it still exist, and the concrete roof that collapsed, like a tiger's back or an ocean wave, lay upon it.

5.

I made my way across the path, which I never crossed before, and I descended, as in those recurrent dreams in which I descend these stairs together with all my friends and all those who are close to me. It's the dream that always takes me back there, when I know that there is no way to avoid that place, that everyone is bound to arrive at that place because it is an inalterable law of the place, one from which there is no escape, and there is no chance for the fantasy we conjure up about liberation and an end, like playful childish fantasies, for an iron law leads everyone there and no one will escape from there.

I also knew, because everyone died one night and I remained, I knew that at the last moment I would be saved. Not for any merit of mine, but because of some sort of inexorable fate. That night dream always brings me back to the same immutable law by which I end up back inside the crematorium and, by some roundabout way, through canals of dark water, through trenches and hidden openings, I dig beneath the barbed wire and reach freedom and board a train, and at one desolate station at night a loudspeaker calls my name, and I am returned to the place I am bound to reach: the crematorium. And however much I know that I must be caught, I always know, too, that I must be spared. It's a kind of circle, a cycle of Tantalus or Sisyphus, or of whatever myth we choose to invoke that is germane here, which returns in an endless vicious circle to the same place.

I decided to descend those stairs. I knew I first had to ascend that broken wave of the roof. I climbed onto it and crossed its entire length, waited there for however long I waited, and finally descended the stairs that led down. I descended stair by stair, in the place where all those whose names and images I remembered had descended, and all those – myriads upon myriads – whom I had seen being swallowed up in endless rows into the crematoria and afterwards I imagined how they rose in fire and flames into the illuminated night sky above the chimneys. Finally I reached the bottom. It was impossible to enter the gas chamber itself, because the roof had collapsed into it and blocked the entrance. So I turned around, finally, and slowly ascended the same stairs.

6.

## *The Way Back*

I emerged from the ruins and made my way to the exit from Birkenau, through the same brick gate by which I had entered. I reached the driver and without a word handed him my old Leica camera, which had accompanied me on my sojourn through these landscapes. He took a picture of the gate with its iron mesh doors, and in front of it, me sliced in two.

Afterwards, without saying a word we left that place.

In the plane, which tossed back and forth – it was a small plane – I wrote some mad things in my diary that I always carry with me. I also wrote them in a letter; I don't know if the letter still exists.

Thus I began to cope with my return, not in a dream but consciously, to the Metropolis of Death.

7.

# 2

# Between Theresienstadt and Auschwitz

The immersion into that time begins between Theresienstadt and Auschwitz. More precisely, it is the onset of the road to the Metropolis of Death. There is no need for me to describe the routine of the transport of the tens of thousands of deportees in the cattle cars, but this case involves a singular episode which I remember and which comes back to me frequently. In the car, we climbed, somehow, my mother and I, to the window, which was blocked with barbed wire, and as we passed through Bohemia in a still unknown direction, mother took out a small notebook she had with her and scribbled a few notes and scattered them to the winds, into the fields. On these scraps of paper she had written the address of my aunt, who was still in Bohemia. I still remember the words: 'We are travelling to the East. We do not know to where. Please, anyone who finds this note, send it to the address above.' The notes arrived. We learned of this after the war. But owing to my aunt's cautiousness they were destroyed upon arrival; none were preserved.

This episode came to mind not long ago, when I read again a short poem written by my friend, the late Dan Pagis, which incorporates it. I do not know whether I told him about it or whether it is one of numberless recurring episodes like it. For him, it occurred between Eve and her son Abel, and the message the passers-by were asked to deliver was intended for her older son, Cain.

Here is the full text of Dan Pagis's poem, which he titled 'Written in Pencil in the Sealed Railway-Car':

here in this carload
i am eve
with abel my son
if you see my other son
cain son of man
tell him that i[1]

## Corridor of Light to the Metropolis of Death

We arrived in Auschwitz. As we began to draw near – of course, we did not know where we were – the first signs were chains of flickering lights, lights hanging from a grid of electrified barbed wire and stooped concrete columns, all fashioned in the same pattern, and the rows – the rows stretched onward, so it seemed to us, for kilometres. All around we saw camp after camp, a grid of rectangles illuminated by lights, and rows of wooden barracks. And as we passed between the camps on that railway track, my mother, who was generally optimistic, understood that this was the --- that from here no one left. Understood that it was something which afterwards, in my private mythology, was given that name, to which I always return, the 'Metropolis of Death'.

By an irony of fate we had volunteered of our own will, my mother and I – I was ten at the time – to leave Theresienstadt in favour of Auschwitz, because her mother – my grandmother – together with her sister and her son, in fact all our entire remaining family there, had to leave on the transport for that unknown place. We volunteered, and I promised my friends in the Theresienstadt children's house that if the new place should turn out to be better, I would write to them. Maybe it would be worth their while to come, too. And in fact some did write from there, postcards, but the postcards people sent – those who sent them – usually tried to intimate to those who remained that, for example, 'every day we meet Onkel Hlad' or 'Onkel Mavet', meaning 'Uncle Starvation' in Czech or 'Uncle Death' in Hebrew.

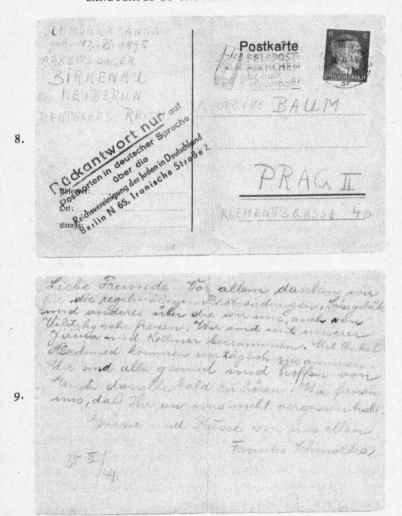

8.

9.

I return to the first hour of our arrival. This scene of night, of the darkness, of the lights, of that horizon-to-horizon grid of columns and barbed wire, is one of the recurring images engraved upon me, and I develop them and build them in my imagination, either in dreams or in particular situations in which I plunge back into that time. This remains perhaps the freshest symbol, if one can say so, of that fresh night with the fresh lights, when the convoy, weary to death, thirsty to death, reached the gates of that Metropolis.

## The 'Family Camp' – the Riddle of its Exemption from the Order of the 'Final Solution'

Within a short time we found ourselves in one of the camps. All of us were there – women, children, the elderly. It was not until a few days later that we learned that a miracle had occurred, a miracle whose meaning no one understood. On that ramp, on that railway station platform onto which we stepped, every transport of deportees was received at Auschwitz with the same well-known procedure – the selection – after which most of the new arrivals were sent to the gas chambers and the minority, those who were fit for work, were sent, after disinfection and a change of clothes into prisoner's garb, to one of the labour camps inside Auschwitz. In our case, we were all sent to one camp, our heads were not shaved, we were allowed to keep our own clothes, and the veteran inmates who visited the camp explained to us that this was a great mystery, which none of them could fathom.

Among the veteran inmates who visited that camp shortly after our arrival in September 1943 was one who had been in concentration camps since 1939 and in Auschwitz since 1942. I mean my father. He found us, identified us among the arrivals from Theresienstadt – he knew we would come from Theresienstadt – looked for us, for my mother and me, and explained to my mother, and in fact to all the inmates, the meaning of the scenes that had occurred on the platform, with the daily arrival of trainloads of prisoners, who were sorted into groups and then advanced slowly in long processions toward brick buildings with large smokestacks which spew flames and smoke day and night; explained to us about selections, about crematoria, about gas chambers – explained about Auschwitz-Birkenau, the very heart of the event whose roots and development I traced, perhaps not willingly, many years later.

What was this camp, which was officially called BIIb but which the inmates referred to as *Familienlager*, because whole families were housed there, unlike in the other camps? What was the meaning of this 'miracle'? What was the purpose of this camp? No one ever found out, not even after the camp was liquidated. A liquidation that was carried out the hard way, harder perhaps than according to 'standard procedure' in Auschwitz. I described all this in an article, perhaps the only article I devoted to the subject of the concentration camps, all of course based on documentation I found in German archives. In the article I use the third person, as one who is describing a distant historical reality.[2] But there are things the article does not speak of, which remain with me as potent experiences. Some of them arise in my memory more frequently, others less so.

## The Youth and Children's Block

The initial memory is of the first days, when amid the terrible chaos of the inmates inside the barracks and the unmade dirt path someone appeared whom we knew well from Theresienstadt. His name was Fredy Hirsch, a man of prestige and authority among the youth, a *madrich*,[3] an athlete, whose exploits we still remembered from when we had been together at the Theresienstadt ghetto. He was now supposed to be appointed an Auschwitz-style Kapo in this camp. To everyone's surprise, he asked to be released from that post and to engage in something else, which immediately became clear to us. He gathered all the children and youth in one large structure – or 'block', as it was known there – and devoted both himself and the team of *madrichim* he chose to educating and looking after the youngsters. Within a short time this barracks became the centre of the spiritual and cultural life of the place. I say this in the full sense of the words: it was a place where plays were staged and concerts performed – and all this, of course, a hundred and fifty to two hundred metres from the selection platform and three hundred to four hundred metres from the crematoria. The experiences that I remember from there unquestionably form the moral basis for my approach to culture, to life, almost to everything, as it took shape within me during those few months, at the age of ten and eleven, between September 1943 and the camp's liquidation in July 1944.

What do I remember from that block? First, what I do not remember. Not long ago, I met one of the boys who was with me in the same barracks. He now lives in Australia. The question that bothered him, he told me, was whether, when we had classes there, we sat on benches or on the dirt floor. He could remember neither what we learned nor how we learned, but it was the visual aspect that haunted him. Try as I might, I could not dredge up this information from my memory. I could not remember whether there were benches or a dirt floor. When I tried to visualize benches, what suddenly came to mind were the benches in the dining hall of the kibbutz in Israel, and I understood that it was not from there. I remembered that floor, but it was one of the first images of the barracks that I saw, immediately after our arrival.

What I recall with greater clarity is our first history lesson. There I heard for the first time about the riveting developments in the Battle of Thermopylae and about the whole constellation of wars between the Persians and the Greeks. I also remember being so fascinated by this that I took in almost every word in the lessons, and when an inspector arrived – there was in fact a self-created inspection unit that monitored the pupils' progress – I, the smallest of the lot, rattled off the whole collection of those fascinating stories about the First and Second Persian Wars, the great naval battle at Salamis, the Battle of Thermopylae, and the thrilling message of the Marathon runner ... That was not a deep experience – I had deeper and stronger experiences – but it was, I think, the first one from there. Sometimes I chuckle to myself when I consider the possibility that the encounter which perhaps destined me for the profession which as a young man, when I arrived at the university, I at first saw no point or purpose in pursuing – the study of history – had its roots in that formative experience. Possibly.

What was far more exciting, and stuck more powerfully, is that artistic performances took place in the block and that we participated in them. One of them, the most grandiose, was an entire children's opera which we performed there. I remember taking part in many rehearsals. I did not see the performance itself, because I was by then in the hospital, ill with diphtheria. It was all very thrilling, because of the tremendous effort involved in preparing the texts – in

German – the recitatives and the singing, together with the rest of the preparations, including wall paintings.

10.

But what sticks in my memory even more are the skits in which I took part. Each group undertook to present an imaginary future situation that was grounded in the Auschwitz reality. I no longer remember all the shows in detail, but I do remember those sarcasms, which both the children and the instructors understood well. Our group presented 'Heavenly Auschwitz – Earthly Auschwitz': as newcomers in Heaven, we discovered to our astonishment that in the world on high there were selections and there were crematoria. Or in another scene of the performance: to the astonishment of the surgeon operating in Heavenly Auschwitz the same lice, the Auschwitz epidemics' emissaries of death, were discovered in the patient's intestines.

Something else I remember well is that SS men also attended the performances, as spectators. Among them was Doctor Mengele and another physician named Lucas – I later testified against him in the Auschwitz trial in Frankfurt. The cryptic hints, the coded language enabled us – children and *madrichim* alike – to give expression to the

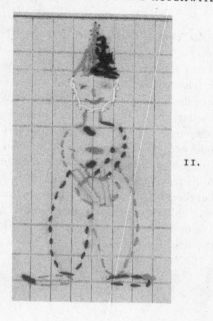

II.

two facets of our situation. Whether those spectators got the message or not, it was important for us. That special humour, that black humour with which we made jokes, even without shows, about the only way one left Auschwitz – through its smokestacks, the smokestacks of the crematoria – jokes in this vein, or the language we developed as our vernacular, was a constant work in progress that was created there, and I can remember nothing like it from this point of view at any stage of my life. I did not use that language with more than one person, perhaps two, among the closest to me here in Jerusalem, long after the war: with one of the youths who was with me there, the painter Yehuda Bacon; and with my best friend, the late German-language poet Gerschon Ben-David, who learned all the coded idioms of that ironical way of speech, enabling us to conduct a kind of 'amusing' dialogue of unique black humour.

## The Great Death and the Small Death

There were other amusements in that camp, too. As children, we were very curious to know whether the barbed wire of the electrified fence was really electrified. The question gave us no rest. We would approach the fence – by day, not at night – and compete among ourselves over who would dare to touch the barbed wire and stay alive.

For the most part, the fence was not electrified during the day. Our fear was great, but so too was our need to overcome this small fear. To overcome the great fear of the crematoria and of the immutable law that led to them was impossible. The victory over this grid by the daring of small children, who took a deliberate risk in order to test this subsystem of death – the fence, which was not intended to kill other than in particular situations – was in itself a great thing.

12.

Those were extracurricular amusements, unrelated to 'the block'. Less amusing were sights which I took in only rarely, or only rarely, apparently, allowed myself to take in. These were heaps of bodies, which are very difficult to describe: only skin and bones. Skeletons covered only by yellow skin. The skeletons were removed from the barracks at night by the back door and were later collected. We lived in a kind of hothouse in that children's block, but at night we slept with our parents; I with my mother. Every morning I encountered the same scenes. I always passed them quickly, but they stayed with me.

A great many other things did not stay. If we consider the entire Auschwitz universe, to its farthest reaches, as a youth I did not feel the acute, murderous, destructive discord and torment felt by every adult inmate who was uprooted and wrenched from his cultural world and its norms and hurled into a confrontation with norms of cruelty, of death. In my case, that discord, experienced by every adult inmate who remained alive, and which was almost always one of the elements of the shock that often felled them within a short time, did not exist, because this was the first world and the first order I had ever known: the order of the selections, death as the sole certain perspective ruling the world. All this was almost self-evident. I had longings, I will not say I did not, I had longings to suddenly return home, to that haven and to that lost freedom, whose loss I felt already in Theresienstadt, when I stood on the fortified walls and gazed at the distant blue vistas beyond, now out of reach. The difference was that here, unlike in Theresienstadt, it was also clear that no one would leave this place alive. Death was a basic given, its dominion over every person not in doubt.

As I said, that sharp confrontation did not take the same form in me, at least not in that block, in which I encountered history for the first time, music almost for the first time, and also death; and also the skeletons, and also the selections, which we saw from afar, and we knew; and also those images which preoccupied me, disturbed me, but were part of the day-to-day reality: the images, particularly toward evening, as dark descended slowly across the skies of Poland, when we watched the crematoria burning with a quiet constant fire, and the flames a few metres high rising above the red-brick chimneys of the crematoria, and the smoke billowing and rising above the flames, and the riddle that engaged us, me especially: how does it happen that the living, who enter in their masses in long columns and are swallowed into these structures made of sloping roofs and red bricks, are transformed into flames, into light and smoke, then disappear and

13.

fade into those darkening skies? In the star-strewn night sky, too, the fire continues to burn, quietly. That belonged to everyday life. Yet nevertheless, the riddle of life, curiosity about life and death of this sort, somehow was rife within us.

## 'Ode to Joy'

There were things that were quite extraordinary in that camp, which are part of my private mythology and have remained lodged in some corner of my memory and flutter around there in one form or another. One of them – and I am not talking now about the mass liquidation and the events that determined the fate of everyone, but about myself – one of them, which was particularly bizarre, crystallized in my memory, or took shape in my memory, entered my memory in two very peculiar stages in the life of that camp. In the children's barracks there was a choir conductor. His name, as I recall, was Imre.[4] A big man; quite huge. He organized a children's choir and we held rehearsals. I don't remember if we also gave performances as a choir, though it was not as part of the opera, which was another matter. The rehearsals almost always took place in one of the long halls. I mean one of the long barracks that were used as lavatories for prisoners, pipes with holes drilled in them running along about fifty metres of the structure – an excellent German invention that I came across once later on, after the war, in the public toilet of the Friedrichstrasse station in East Berlin, immediately after I arrived there. Within seconds the sight took me back to that place in Auschwitz. But that is something else.

That barracks had exceptional acoustics – when there were no prisoners there, of course. In the morning or in the evening, after work, it was packed with thousands, but during the day it was empty. There, in the autumn months – we arrived in September – in the autumn and winter months of 1943 we held the rehearsals. I remember mainly one work that we sang and I also remember the words. The words had to do with joy and with the brotherhood of man. They made no special impression on me, and I am sure I would have forgotten all this completely had it not been for another incident in which the experience and the melody and the text came back. About half a year later, when the camp no longer existed, when most of its prisoners had already been cremated or sent as slaves across the Reich, and only a few dozen of the youths remained and we had been moved to the *Männerlager*, the large slave camp, a harmonica somehow came into my possession. I learned to play it and I played things that entered my mind, including one of the melodies we sang in the children's choir. It goes something like this:

I am playing the melody in one of those rare moments of quiet and tranquillity in that camp, and a young Jewish prisoner from Berlin comes up to me – I was then a boy of eleven – and says: 'Do you know what you are playing?' And I tell him: 'Look, what I am playing is a melody we sang in that camp – which no longer exists.' He then explained to me what I was playing and what we sang there and the meaning of those words. I think he also tried to explain the terrible absurdity of it, the terrible wonder of it, that a song of praise to joy and to the brotherhood of man, Schiller's 'Ode to Joy' from Beethoven's Ninth Symphony, was being played opposite the crematoria of Auschwitz, a few hundred metres from the place of execution, where the greatest conflagration ever experienced by that same mankind that was being sung about was going on at the very moment we were talking and in all the months we were there.

Actually, by then I already knew about Beethoven. I had not known when we had sung him. Between that first occasion, when we sang, and the surprising discovery and identification of the melody, I had been in the hospital, ill with diphtheria, and on the pallet above me was one of the young prisoners, about twenty years old. His name was Herbert. I think he did not get well, and if he did get well he ended up where so many others did in the Metropolis of Death. One of our amusements, though mainly his, was to explain to me, or convey to me, something of the cultural riches he had accumulated, as though he were bequeathing me that legacy. The first thing I got from him was a book, the only book he possessed, and I would read it. It opens with a description of an old woman and a young man who strikes her with an axe, who murders and is tormented – Dostoevsky's *Crime and Punishment*. That was what he took to Auschwitz and that was the first work of great literature I read since I was cut off from my parents' library in Czechoslovakia at the age of nine. It didn't stop with Dostoevsky. We went on to Shakespeare and Beethoven and Mozart and whatever he could cram into me of European culture. And I took in quite a bit.

When Schiller and Beethoven were afterwards identified, I began to ponder, and I have pondered ever since, the reasons and the meaning of that decision by the conductor, that Imre, whom I remember as though it were today, as a large, awkward figure in the blue-grey prisoner's uniform and the big wooden shoes, with the big hands of a conductor, urging on the choir, making it come together and then loosening his hold, and we are singing like little angels, our voices providing an accompaniment to the processions of the people in black who are slowly swallowed up into the crematoria.

Naturally, the question I asked myself, and that I go on asking myself to this day, is what drove that Imre – not to organize the children's choir, because after all one could say that in the spirit of that project of the educational centre it was necessary somehow to preserve sanity, somehow to keep occupied – but what he believed. What was his intention in choosing to perform that particular text, a text that is considered a universal manifesto of everyone who believes in human dignity, in humanistic values, in the future – facing those crematoria, in the place where the future was perhaps the only definite thing that did not exist? Was it a kind of protest demonstration, absurd perhaps, perhaps without any purpose, but an attempt not to forsake and not to lose, not the belief in, but the devotion to those values which ultimately only the flames could put an end to – only that fire, and not all that preceded it raging around us; that is, as long as man breathes he breathes freedom, something like that?

That is one possibility, a very fine one, but there is a second possibility, which is apparently far more likely, or may sometimes be called for. I will not say when I prefer the first and when I am inclined to the other. I refer to the possibility that this was an act of extreme sarcasm, to the outermost possible limit, of self-amusement, of a person in control of naive beings and implanting in them naive values, sublime and wonderful values, all the while knowing that there is no point or purpose and no meaning to those values. In other words, that this was a kind of almost demonic self-amusement of playing melodies to accompany those flames that burned quietly day and night and those processions being swallowed into the insatiable crematoria.

The second notion seems more logical on the face of it. The first notion is very tempting to believe in. And maybe I believe in it, maybe it influenced me, maybe it influenced a great deal of what I am occupied with and believe in. But there are many times when I think I cling to an illusion and pass it on in various ways. Because that abysmal, ultimate sarcasm, beyond any possible limit, could also be a criterion for less extreme variations in the reality of a world where things do not proceed according to the unreserved belief of Beethoven

14.

and Schiller as such, but Beethoven and Schiller who had once been sung opposite the Auschwitz crematoria. That is of course part of my private mythology.

I often come back to all that and it also occupies me professionally, even though I never mention the episode directly. But when I come to interpret the continuity of the existence of social norms, of cultural and moral values in the conditions that were created immediately upon the Nazis' ascent to power and all the way to the brink of the mass-murder pits and the crematoria, here I am very often inclined, perhaps unconsciously, to choose the belief in that demonstration, a hopeless demonstration but the only possible one in that situation, though I think, as I said, that the illusion here is sometimes far greater than the fierceness of the sarcasm or the cynical amusement of one who was still able to toy with it in the face of that mass death. That approach was perhaps more – I will not say more realistic – but more authentic.

The subject remains an open one for me, like Imre's big arms that opened to both sides and hung there. Whoever chooses the left or the right, or when I choose the left or the right, that is in fact the whole unfolding of my existence or of my confrontation both with the past and with the present from then until today.

# 3

# Final Liquidation of the 'Family Camp'

At the end of six months, in the course of one night, all five thousand, or all who remained of the five thousand who arrived with us in September 1943, were annihilated. On that night in March 1944, nearly all of them died in the gas chambers, apart from a few who only by chance happened to be hospitalized and were left alive in order to deceive the others – the doctors and the patients – my mother and I among them. Those who arrived in later transports knew that, like their predecessors, they had about six months left to live. Why? No one knew. When I returned from the hospital, the whole life of the camp was conducted under the certain knowledge that, like the inexorable sands of an hourglass, the days were running out and would end in the crematoria.

The liquidation began in July, this time differently. Everyone in the camp underwent a 'regular' selection, the conventional way at Auschwitz. Those fit for work were sent to labour camps in Germany – my mother was among them – the others to the gas chambers. I was one of those others, designated to die by gas, for the second time. The first time I had come through by chance, but the second time chance did not appear on the horizon until, once more in an unexpected way, the end was postponed. After the selections were concluded, an order arrived to choose several dozen youths for work in the camp, such as hauling carts, because, after all, manpower was cheaper than horses, which were a precious commodity. Accordingly, we were transferred to a different camp and thus eluded this stage of the liquidation of the family camp.

# 'The Eternal Death of the Child – the Eternal Death and Resurrection of the Great Death'

These things are bound up with several situations which recur within a kind of mythic dreamscape. That night in March, in which all my childhood friends – and part of my family, as I discovered the following morning – were annihilated, comes back in images which I did not see with my own eyes but which I continually re-experience. How they enter the gas chambers and I with them, because I belong to them. How they and I enter the corridor and afterwards the gas chambers and I with them. And how I at the last minute, by some roundabout way, escape – once through the opening created when a small, rusting iron door opens, another time through some sort of subterranean stream of water – and I come out of the crematorium and dig beneath the barbed wire. Numberless images like this.

On one occasion I deliver a speech to the youths in the block, trying to persuade them that, even though the place to which we are to be taken has been described to us as a labour camp, this is no more than an exercise in deception, and in fact we are condemned to die. When we arrive there I somehow slip away, I do not go with them, I escape alone. I know – as we approach the place – that I will escape – or, actually, not that I will escape but that at the last minute events will not sweep me up. This basic certainty – wholly rational – that the only way out of here is the gas, the suffocation and the fire, is so powerful that it is impossible not to believe in this. And nonetheless I believe.

This is a concrete situation which recurred several times in Auschwitz itself and returns paradigmatically, as dreams, whether of escape or return; escape by train, the image of a deserted night station, when suddenly the loudspeakers call my name and I report and am sent back to Auschwitz, to the crematoria; and I know there is no escaping them and that the only way and the only law that governs them is the fulfilment of an imperative and resignation to death and annihilation. Yet I also know that at the last minute somehow I will not become enmeshed in that immutable law, that here something is different. This is a hope which, though I do not believe in it, is always present and in the end becomes certainty, rife with fear and torments – not torments but terror and feverish flight and feverish extrication in one way or another – and all recurring in numberless variations.

15.

In Auschwitz itself I underwent the experience concretely, a number of times. The second time was when we, a group of youths, left the camp, knowing that the camp administration often misled people and reassured them, in order to avert attempts at rebellion by veteran inmates who knew what the road to the crematoria meant. We were told that we must go through the 'sauna camp' – a camp where body and clothing of the arriving inmates were disinfected – and then go on to the main camp. We left our camp; it was the first time we had passed through the gates of the camp. We turned left and drew ever closer to one of the crematoria. We were all unendurably tense. The feeling that this immutability of the law, of liquidation, of annihilation, would devolve on us was stupendous, overpowering. The hope that perhaps, after all, we were not being tricked, was there. It was searing, feverish, but very hesitant, and with every step that brought us closer to the crematorium the horror mounted. The black gates, the fences we could not see over, filled us with dread. The prisoners, who came from every corner of Europe, stood and waited for hours. Few knew what awaited them – but we knew, we knew all about this 'industry'.

16.

We gazed at the smokestacks of one of the crematoria there. Step by step we drew closer. That primal experience of looming horror and of being sucked into it, swallowed within it – that is what persisted; that, and not the relief, the overwhelming feeling of relief as we walked past the gate and continued toward the 'sauna camp' and entered it and through the windows could even see into the crematorium compound – all this I somehow remember, but this experience did not persist in the memory. The primal experience, the one that persisted, is the trauma, recurring numberless times and encapsulating, like a highly concentrated essence, the immutable law of the Great Death. A law that prevailed and applied to each and every one of us. Grappling with it – hopelessly – yet aspiring compulsively to escape its clutches, was a formative experience.

# The 'Small Death' and the 'Life beyond Death'

A completely different type of encounter with the Auschwitz form of death lay in a kind of development, if one can put it like that, an involuntary upgrading of the games of daring, the games of touching the electrified barbed-wire fence. This was in October 1944. By then I was already in the men's camp together with my father, working as an apprentice to a group of blacksmiths, of whom my father was one. Every day after work I would pass a small metal container of soup to my uncle through the barbed wire. The uncle, my mother's brother, had arrived from Theresienstadt and was in an adjacent camp. That particular day, around dusk, was the same. But on that day a revolt broke out among the *Sonderkommando* inmates in one of the crematoria, an event which became fateful for me as well. The inmates rebelled, set fire to the crematorium, and tried to escape. The procedure in such cases was to electrify the fence. Of course, I did not learn about all this until afterwards.

As I did every day, I passed the container with the soup through the fence, and at one point I touched the barbed wire. I felt shocks run through every part of my body and I was stuck to the fence. I was immobilized but felt as though I had risen into the air and was floating a few centimetres above the ground. At that moment I understood well what had happened: I was caught on the electrified fence.

At that moment it was also clear to me that I was dead, because it was known that anyone caught on the wire died instantly. But I see, even as I float, even as I experience a choking feeling, as I look at the world around me – I see that nothing has changed. Blue skies hide between the clouds, there are people opposite me – opposite me, wearing a faded green coat and holding a large wooden pole, a Soviet prisoner of war was standing and staring. The only thought that kept pounding in my head the whole time was: I am dead, and the world as I see it has not changed! Is this what the world looks like after death?

Here was the boundless curiosity a human being possesses from the moment he first becomes aware of his mortality; curiosity that

17.

transcends death: 'What is it like to be dead? Is this what it is like to be dead? After all, one sees the world as it is and the world is open before me. I am floating, yes, but nothing has changed.' This riddle, which had vexed me since the age of five or six, without any connection to death or to the Metropolis of Death or to the crematoria, was suddenly solved. Death is not death – the world has not changed; I see the world and I take in the world. That was the experience that overwhelmed me during all those long minutes and seconds, until someone standing there grabbed the wooden pole – or maybe it was a shovel – from the Soviet prisoner of war and poked me in the chest with it a few times. I slid to the ground.

What happened afterwards – that is a different story. The burns on my hands turned into pus-filled sores and I had to hide to avoid being selected for the group of those unfit for work . . .

# 4

# Autumn 1944: Auschwitz –
# Ghostly Metropolis

After the *Sonderkommando* uprising, and my personal episode on the barbed wire, came the great evacuation of Auschwitz. Most of the remaining inmates underwent selection. The result was that almost everyone departed. This selection was intended less for annihilation than to choose those who were fit to leave Auschwitz for forced labour in Germany. Train after train, column after column of veteran inmates and all the types of prisoners who were still among the living set out for camps in Germany. The evacuation of Auschwitz had begun. It was clear: everyone who remained faced a certain end. Those who left embarked on a road of great uncertainty, but one that was an exit from the closed circle. Almost all of my father's friends, and the two of us also, did all we could to be included among those who were to leave. I would not have got through the selection – because of my burned hands and my age – but, as I had the last time, during the evacuation of the camp of the Theresienstadt Jews, I stole into the men's group and joined them on the way to the gate and the trains.

## The Recurring Return from the
## Gates of the Camp

At the gate I was sent back. It was almost a repeat of the previous episode, when I attached myself to the youth group. I was a few years younger than the others and it was obvious that I had no chance to get through the gate. The guard was a terrifying SS man named Buntrock whom we children, like the other inmates, called Bulldog.

Through this gate, under his watchful eye, everyone passed, one by one, and when I got there he asked me: 'How old are you?' 'Fifteen,' I replied. He said: '*Warum lügst du?*' – 'Why are you lying?' – I was barely eleven and a half. There was nothing I could say. I knew what I knew before I got there. I came to that exit point when it was time for this great immutable law – that no one gets away from here – a law that applied also to me, to be realized, and by being sent back I would join those who were condemned to be incorporated in the immutable law of death, the law of the Great Death, the immutable law that governs this Metropolis of Death and is indeed finally being realized at this stage. Because, after this stage there is no more death.

18.

Buntrock, *Fritz, Wilh.*

This Buntrock, who was known for his cruelty, hesitates a moment and then swings his large hand toward me, points toward the group of youths, and says: '*Hau ab!*' – 'Scram!'

He sends me to join the rest of the youths, setting in motion the terrible journey of fear I have already described, toward the crematoria: left into the crematoria or straight ahead to the next stage, perhaps, to another camp inside Auschwitz and new ordeals and struggles that will delay the fulfilment of the immutable law for a short time. I have no idea what his reasons and considerations were – maybe something moved inside him, maybe he wanted to avoid the bother of a recount – it is certainly not relevant to my inner experience. It was clear to me that the implementation of the immutable law, by which I too was incorporated in the unfolding scheme of the Great Death, had been deferred.

Well, that miracle did not recur in the great evacuation of Auschwitz in the autumn of 1944: I was sent back. My time, it was plain to me, had come. Attempts at escape were done with; petty struggles gave way to resignation to the immutable law of the Great Death and the inevitable end. Thereafter, in the months that remained until the final liquidation in January, Auschwitz became a ghost camp and life proceeded ineluctably on borrowed time. It was plain to all who remained that their borrowed time would run out upon the approach of the front line and the camp's final liquidation.

This last return from the camp's exit gate was far more fraught than all the previous stages of the struggles, survivals and hopes with their panoply of experiences. For here, accompanying that searing personal fear – as potent as my terror of death – was the feeling that the overriding law and order that governs all these realms was about to be realized. It was like facing the full rigour of the law, a kind of terrible justice crushing small wrongs in the grinder of all-surpassing wrong that lies beyond.

Many years later, here in Jerusalem, when I read the stories of Kleist, it seemed to me that I understood cognitively what I had then intuited. I understood the great and terrible impulse toward such returning and resignation, or perhaps attachment to returning and resignation to order and to the terrifying law beyond. In *Michael Kohlhaas* and in *The Earthquake in Chile* it was the immutable law that was bound to be realized, against which every revolt always remains no more than a small, desperate, hopeless deferment.

Auschwitz as a ghost camp in autumn 1944, or from autumn 1944 until January 1945, when the final evacuation took place, was arrestingly different from what it had been before. With the annihilation terminated and the crematoria having ceased to operate, there ended also the long columns of people in black being swallowed up in the furnaces, ended also the movement of the trains and no more piles of last possessions of the deportees. The flames ceased. Only one fire continued to flicker, consuming those who died a 'natural death'.

Nevertheless, things continued to happen. Most significantly, the crematoria began to be dismantled and the remaining structures were blown up. That produced a strange feeling, but in truth it did not call into question anything about that ever-present sense of certainty about the Great Death, about the immutable law of the Great Death. Not the one that swallows those who come from every corner of Europe, but the one that devolves on the inhabitants of the Metropolis. As for them, their fate was sealed – that was my feeling always.

Then winter arrived, from afar we could hear the thunder of the cannons of the approaching front, and the order was given to move from the Birkenau camp, which lay in the heart of the annihilation machine, to Auschwitz I camp, where political prisoners were incarcerated. From there, on the night of 18 January, began the journey, through the gates that were opened, to a kind of freedom, into the white snow, the night snow, into expanses dispossessed of all the accoutrements of that Metropolis I knew, which I had breathed every moment since coming to it on that night of flickering chains of light.

## The Other Night Journey

The feeling of amazement, of puzzlement, was far more powerful than the feeling of a prospect of freedom, a possibility of rescue. But for me there was something new, something odd about these broad expanses which stretched in every direction – the snow's whiteness, the trees, the villages, and alongside the slow movement of the prisoners' march there occasionally appeared those dark stains whose meaning I did not at first fathom. At first there was a feeling that this might be a journey of human rivers, flowing and breaching the Metropolis of Death, the boundaries of the Metropolis of Death, the gates of the Metropolis of Death to – perhaps – some distant freedom. But the dark stains, it soon became apparent, were death's drips onto the white snow, coiling all who went by into some dark chain, constantly expanding and overtaking the human rivers that wound slowly forward. Within a short time it became clear to me that every black stain was a prisoner who had been shot and dumped by the roadside. Whoever lagged behind, unable to keep pace with the march, was shot. Ever more people passed from the side of the living to the side of the black stains, and from a dark trickle there formed a stream alongside the rivers, the columns, from which freedom constantly receded.

This episode of the death march is an event in its own right, the escape and the rescue alike, but this is not the place to describe it.

For me, that journey ended as something which never actually arrived at freedom. I remained in that Metropolis, a prisoner of that Metropolis, of that immutable law which leaves no place for being rescued, for violating this terrible 'justice' by which Auschwitz must remain Auschwitz. Thus the immutable law remained for me and thus did I remain caught up within it, which was actually what I discovered when I returned decades later. In that return, with the completion of the last act, which I had not then been 'privileged' to experience – the act of descending into the ruins that survived, at least to those of the gas chamber of the crematorium – that immutable law ran its course, the Kleistian or indeed Kulkaesque 'crowning glory was restored' and closes the odyssey in which I remained yoked and bound to that place.

# 5

# Observations and Perplexities about Scenes in the Memory

I turn now to a question which occupies me a great deal, in particular when I listen to these recordings and when I read the descriptions I set down in my diaries of the landscapes of the Metropolis of Death. The pervasive, all-governing element in them is the immutable law, utterly impersonal, of the Great Death. In contrast there are the more personal games of the 'small death'. Almost absent – in truth, completely absent – is another element, so well known from the memoirs and testimonies about daily life in the concentration camps. I mean the violence, the cruelty, the torture, the individual killings, which, as far as I can make out – though I generally avoid reading such texts – are portrayed as the everyday routine of that world of the camps. I am obliged to ask myself whether anything of that violence, anything of that violence and cruelty remains in my memory. (I almost said my memoirs, but I am engaged in probing the memory, not writing memoirs.) What's puzzling is that I possess almost no such memories; I have to think hard and scan the images that remain engraved in one form or another – as experiences, as colours, as impressions – in order to isolate in them something of a type that I could describe as violence.

## 'In the Penal Colony'

Actually, certain episodes of this kind do inhabit my consciousness. Earlier, I described, in passing, the piles of skeletons, the bodies – bones covered with skin – which were heaped up behind the barracks before dawn and which we children sidestepped, skirted, on the way to the youth barracks in the special camp of the Theresienstadt Jews in Auschwitz. In truth, from that camp I remember not one scene of violence, though violence there certainly was, as is apparent from the drawings by Dinah Gottlieb and from many other descriptions which my friend, the poet Gerschon Ben-David, recorded from older inmates.

19.

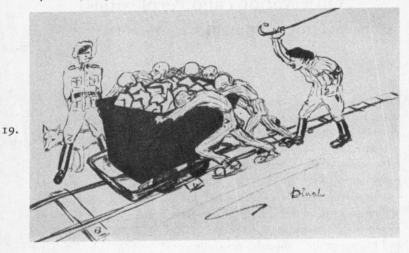

I neither wrote down nor recorded any of this from memory as testimony for its own sake. So it seems to me at this moment.

Nevertheless, one salient episode is sharply etched in my mind in every detail: an act of public punishment. An incident in which a prisoner was punished in the presence of the other prisoners – they were forced to watch. This was in the autumn of 1944, in the men's camp, after the liquidation of the family camp; in the camp that was the centre of Birkenau, the main labour camp, the camp of the veteran prisoners, the new inmates, and of us youths as well. The recollection perhaps dredges up something additional from that period, the period after the massive evacuation of Auschwitz, which was then being implemented, from autumn to winter 1944, as though by inertia. There was something of a ghostly atmosphere about it, and as such it remained lodged in my memory.

It was in the morning, early in the morning, 9 o'clock perhaps. An autumnal day on which a kind of haze hung in the air, like a mist. Up close, visibility was fine, clear, but the landscape of hills in the distance, and even the adjacent camps, somehow disappeared. On that foggy morning a surprise search was carried out, a check to find inmates who had shirked work. After all the inmates had left for work outside or inside the camp, everyone who remained inside was ordered to gather for a form of roll-call, an *Appell* in the camp terminology, in the large plaza at the edge of the camp, which faced the ramp, the railway line and the crematoria. The inmates gathered in a large square, row upon row, to the centre of which was led an inmate, someone unknown to me, wearing a prisoner's uniform. He had been caught in the mass latrine, where prisoners sometimes hid. It was close by. He was brought there by a few SS men and was also, as I recall, escorted by a few Kapos who were present at this ceremony of public punishment.

The ceremony began with a kind of game, as though an amusement, in which the SS men beat the prisoner with their walking sticks, though I took in only the victim's bald head, the blows raining down on his skull, the red marks that appeared after each blow. Everything proceeded as though in silence, soundlessly, in the haze-drenched air, yet everything was also perfectly clear and close up, every detail visible. The prisoner, with a kind of grotesque, bizarre dance, tries to dodge the blows and to hold the places where they landed. The blows rained down from every side and always in their wake the red marks on his head. As though it were some sort of game. The impression imprinted in my memory – without any moral consciousness of the act of torture – remained only as an image in my mind's eye: the game of sticks played by the SS men in green, the Kapos in their ironed prisoner's garb, the inmate, head shaven, clad in a foul inmate's uniform, being beaten and tortured. Of his whole being I actually took in only one part: the whiteness of the skull on which the red marks welled and the blood that streamed down his face.

After this foreplay, the prisoner was tied to a special whipping device. His legs were bound and his hands were stretched out in front and also bound. I think it was the Kapos who tied him to the post, while the SS men stood to the side. Then began the second stage of the ceremony: the flogging, each lash counted out by the prisoner himself, one by one. So it is that I remember those lashes, one after the other, and the counting that continued, becoming ever more feeble until it finally fell silent. Afterwards – so I still remember – he was cut loose from the post and everyone dispersed.

What I retain from this scene comes down to a feeling of a peculiar 'justice' that resided in all this; a feeling that it was some sort of actualization of a perplexing 'order' that overlay the camp's everyday life. Victim and perpetrators, or the floggers and the lashes of justice to which the prisoner was sentenced, were as though one system, in which it was impossible to distinguish, to separate the victim from the deliverers of the punishment.

I probably would not have recalled this incident, would not have engraved the scene and its import in my memory, had it not loomed before me again much later when I read Kafka's story 'In der Strafkolonie' – 'In the Penal Colony'. Here again it was the sense of a strange 'justice' residing in the unity of opposites, the justice supposedly exclusive to the 'penal colony', the strange world in which the traveller in the story finds himself; and I saw myself as somehow watching from the side, observing how this perverse 'ingenious' machine, the invention of the penal colony's commandant, records with precision in the flesh of the condemned man the measure of punishment he deserves according to those rules of the game. Yes, it was the same feeling of justice, precision and absurdity which characterize the spectacle described in Kafka's story and can be seen as a spectacle of esoteric justice, a spectacle of justice done and sentence executed with the machinery of punishment in a penal system which is its own autonomous entity. As though enfolded in this is some sort of system that can exist without any connection to the strange landscape the traveller chances upon, and can be transposed to the landscape of the camp on that foggy morning, in Auschwitz itself. And from Auschwitz itself, might infiltrate into every possible situation, as though it is an autonomous system, utterly divorced from any feeling of pity, repulsion, cruelty – even the distinction between victim and perpetrator seems to disappear here completely. This was the way I remembered that scene, that scene of violence-as-ritual, as part of the system, not of the Great Death or of the games of the small death, but of everyday life. The daily routine of the system functioning between the Great Death and the liquidation of Auschwitz camp – in the stage of 'Auschwitz as a ghost town'. But also Auschwitz under the dominion of a shadow of its 'glory' – one aspect of this ghost town that still continued to exist, like the penal colony in the Kafka story, already divested of its purpose, of its original 'meaning' when the system was at its apogee, when the penal colony was at its zenith. Something which has seemingly already passed from the world but still exists, and the order exists, the punishment exists, and the victim plays his part with seeming willingness, and the traveller is puzzled and records the events as he sees them. So they are recorded by me.

## The Execution

Another scene from this aspect of violence and cruelty which arises when I scan my memory involves not punishment but killing. More precisely, an execution. A sentence carried out. Once again as a public occasion, attended by all the camp's inmates. This time around dusk, with the thousands gathering at the other end of the camp, the end near the gate, next to the kitchens, in the large plaza at that far end.

There were large plazas at both ends of the camp, and between

20.

them, on both sides of the road that crossed it lengthwise, stood the rows of barracks.

The event was the execution of three or four Russian prisoners of war who had tried to escape. Their attempted escape, like many others, had failed. They were brought back to camp and sentenced to be executed in the presence of the other inmates. This, then, was after work, toward evening, though still in daylight. It was in the summer.

What do I remember from this occasion? First, a great sea of people, arranged in a U formation. Row upon row of prisoners, and in front the gallows, a number of gallows, a platform with gallows and on it several SS men. And the condemned. Silence. Here I remember the silence. It returns me for the blink of an eye to the previous scene: when I summon up that scene in my memory and connect it with this one, it is the great muteness, the tremendous, stunning silence, and in both cases that image of punishment, that dance of torment and the flailing walking sticks – as though it took place in silence, in a vast stillness that prevailed and ruled all. There was silence then. I remember it well.

So, again, the fraught silence, from which came forth – suddenly slicing – the familiar order: '*Mütze-e-e-en ab!*' – 'Caps off!' – and instantly the whole space shone with the light of thousands of shaved skulls. The prisoners, in a motion drilled into them by numberless harassments, removed their caps in swift unison, producing a kind of huge halo that illuminated the first flickers of twilight. And again – silence. Then the prisoners were led to the gallows.

I no longer remember if a verdict was read out, if words were spoken. What I do remember is the act of their being led to the gallows, the knotting of the ropes, the nooses placed around the necks, and their outcry shattering the silence: '*Za Stalina! Za rodinu!*' – 'For Stalin! For the homeland!' – cries of heroism, of resistance.

I remember that as we stood before this last act I lowered my eyes to the ground and refused to look. My second thought was: you must look! You must engrave it in your heart! You must remember it and you must take revenge at the time of justice and retaliation. So I looked straight ahead and was present for the entire duration of the ceremony: the last outcries of the condemned and the silence that prevailed again as the bodies twitched in the nooses. Then all dispersed.

This thought about justice being done transcends the immutable law which prevailed in that place. As though those cries ripped through the present of that time and revealed another dimension, utopian, but at least for a moment a concrete reality, because everyone heard, everyone listened, because everyone contemplated the revenge which was there called by its name. And I interiorized these things.

## 'The Solution of the German Question'

Again I scan my memory and wonder now whether we saw other manifestations of that thought about breaching the present and coping with the immutable law by different means, by means of other types of protest: protest such as the satirical cabaret in the youth barracks of the family camp, the means of the continued upholding of the values we had brought with us from the humanistic heritage. But all that is a different matter. At the time this was not a clear struggle – let us call it political, conceptual – to undermine the immutable law and its governance, or some leap to beyond the end of its rule, which no one rationally believed was possible. But at the moment of the overt protest and the defiant outcry, it was as though I – at least – wanted to prepare myself for that end, as a chance. Of course it was only for a brief moment, a game into which I was swept, but the cause was real: the desire to retaliate, the desire to take revenge, the desire to see a different reality which would come afterwards. For an instant it was concrete.

Once more, though, I return to the question: it was, after all, a very brief episode, only minutes, yet it remained engraved in my memory, with all the external trappings of the SS men on the platform, the prisoners, this great ceremoniousness. Nevertheless, at the crux of the experience there remained that outcry, that thought, and the reflections of the boy who gazed upon it unflinchingly.

But I return to the question: were there other moments like this, other similar manifestations that I remember which subvert the immutable law? In the strangest way, this search through the recesses of memory – so distinctive and so selective, apparently, in the way these images from the Metropolis lodged in my consciousness – leads me to another formative experience: an encounter with the humanistic heritage of European culture. I fell ill at that time with a disease which seemed to be mortal and was hospitalized in the 'sick people's block' together with a few other critically ill inmates – an episode I described earlier.

Of the other inmates there I remember well the young man with a lean face and the bristles of a beard, named Herbert, and a friend of his. It was Herbert who gave me a copy of Dostoevsky's *Crime and Punishment*, Herbert who explained to me who Beethoven was, and Goethe, and Shakespeare, and about the culture they bequeathed us – that is, European humanism. Herbert and his friend used to entertain themselves during the long hours and days when they were in that place (and I do not know if they came out of there) with a variety of intellectual diversions. One of the things I recall well, though I did not really grasp its meaning at the time, was a game of suggesting ideas for the 'solution of the German question'. The term 'Final Solution of the Jewish Question' was not known then, but the 'solution of the Jewish question' was a very familiar concept. It was obviously a paraphrase, an improvised reversal of fates and – whether I wish to admit it or not – an attempt to retaliate, to bring history to justice, perhaps to avenge the 'solution', which we now term the attempt to implement the 'Final Solution' – the total annihilation of the Jewish people – occurring there before our eyes every day.

The solutions that came up were various and diverse. I remember clearly only one of them. The interesting thing is that it was not an obvious solution, namely, to bring all the members of the German nation to the facilities where the 'solution of the Jewish Question' was taking place: measure for measure. That particular solution was probably the only one that was not put forward. Not the Auschwitz solution, not the solution of annihilation in gas chambers, not a solution of cremation. The solution which I remember well – there were others of its type, too – was to place all the women, the children and the elderly on ships and then sink them in mid-ocean. The men were designated for the kind of slave labour to which we were witness. This I remember, along with the phrase 'the solution of the German question' and the amusement that arose from the wide range of other solutions, which for some reason I do not remember concretely.

Having brought to memory this question – why not Auschwitz? Why not this same Auschwitz, the identical solution? – I can only try to conjecture the answer: possibly this aversion reflected a kind of disgust at contact with the act of murder, the act of execution, the act of annihilation, and was for us at the time a way of denouncing this criminal nation which was responsible for the 'solution of the Jewish Question' in Auschwitz – condemning it, banishing it from the nations of the world and wishing it to disappear into the ocean depths. That was the contrast which seemed to emanate from this bitter amusement, this imagination, this desire for justice to be done, and perhaps also to take revenge. Yes, this I remember.

## 'We, the Dead, Accuse!'

I continue to search and I find the motif of revenge – the motif of the demand for justice to be done, for justice to take its course in due time – in other messages, too: in documents that survived from that place and with which I had direct involvement and contact while still there, still in that Metropolis, and which I actually bore on my body into the post-war world. One is the farewell letter my mother wrote on the night of 30 June 1944, when we thought we would not survive the final liquidation of that camp. She wrote a letter of farewell to my father: a wonderful letter which is now housed in the Yad Vashem Archives after years of being in my father's possession.[1] In one sentence of this letter she expresses outrage at the cruelty of the ordeal: why must the life of an innocent child end by this brutal hand?! And the next sentence resonates with a demand to avenge the guiltless blood, the blood of the innocents that was shed there. At the time, of course, I could not grasp the full implication of this phrase; it was only much later, when I became more familiar with the Jewish tradition, the language of prayer, that I recognized in her words the verse in which the worshippers call on God to avenge the blood of innocents. It seems to me that this sentence resonates with the sense of a call for justice, justice as a meta-dimension, transcending the personal death of family members, unfolding in this prodigious system of the all-ruling Great Death, which cannot be coped with directly. Only by personifying this reality in reference to me – a little boy condemned by that implacable decree to die that night – could she come out with that statement of the call for revenge, for a just reckoning, which must be wrought in some other constellation of history, of thought, of culture, of religion. That verse continually reverberates in my mind: '*Hashem yikom dam nekiim*' – 'God shall avenge the blood of innocents.'

But this was actually an anomaly, a most rare anomaly within the system. Within the system as I remember it, as I experience it unrelentingly. It is the system of the immutable law of the Great Death, an immutability that is seemingly self-enclosed, beyond which lies nothing; and even when there is something like a spark of uprising, of illusion, of hope, such notions only float past here and there like motes on the surface of the grim consciousness that is innate within us. And remains with us afterwards, too, like that system enclosed within itself.

Nevertheless, there were other messages, other sparks that were preserved, some as artistic creation. Like my mother's letter, three other testimonies were also preserved: similar, parallel, but of a quite different type. I am referring to three poems, apparently the last works of an unknown poet of about twenty (her age can be inferred from one of the poems), which were spared extinction on the night of the great annihilation of the members of the transport in which I too arrived in Auschwitz. On that night of the vast conflagration a young woman standing at the entrance to the gas chamber took out, at the last minute, a sheaf of papers and handed them to one of the Kapos, whose task was to ensure that this 'special operation' would be executed 'with no hitches'. The next day he gave my father the pages, knowing that he had ties with the camp of Czech Jews. At first my father thought it was my mother's last regards. Only when he opened the packet did he discover that he was holding the only three poems written in the family camp of the Theresienstadt Jews that survived the flames of Auschwitz. The first one is entitled 'We, the Dead, Accuse!'

# 6

# Three Poems from the Brink of the Gas Chambers

The three poems were written in Czech on thin, faded letter paper. The first of them seems to encapsulate and in its way intensify the message of the three previous episodes I described: the last words of the condemned at their public execution; the sarcastic amusement of the vision of future history according to the condemned in the hospital barracks; and the sentence in my mother's letter demanding revenge for the blood of innocents. But the poems are also more than this, for in all three of them is preserved the only glistening sliver that was saved from a great work of art which existed and perished in that place of perdition.

The first poem, 'We, the Dead, Accuse!', evokes an apocalyptic scene of endless columns of the dead, all bones and ashes, a vast host ever multiplying within the bowels of the earth. In a prophetic vision involving a terrifying resurrection of the dead, the demand is hurled at all of humanity to ensure that justice is done and the final reckoning made.

The second poem, 'Alien Grave', is a lament that does not contain scenes from Auschwitz itself. The poet is keening for an entire historical era in the destiny of Europe, rising in a crescendo of mourning and protest at the pointless mass murder in the two world wars that felled successive generations of Europe's young men.

The third poem, 'I Would Sooner Perish', sets forth a sharp confrontation over the question of responding to violence and bloodshed by means of violence and bloodshed. The last testament of the unknown poet is to choose the way of rejecting violence and of staining her hands with blood, even as resistance in the last hours of those condemned to extinction.

### We, the Dead, Accuse!

No, there are no rotting crosses on our graves
and there are no arching tombstones.
No, there are no wreaths or wrought-metal grilles
or angels with heads inclined,
willows and a wreath with golden thread,
a candle that burns eternally.
We moulder in pits smothered in lime,
the wind rustles in our bones.

Bleached skulls of hopelessness
quiver on the barbed wire
and our ashes go to the four winds
scattered in thousands of urns.

We make a chain around the earth,
seeds dispersed by the winds;
we count the days and years
we wait; time doesn't hurry us.

And there are more and more of us down here;
we swell and grow day by day;
your fields are already bloated with us
and one day your land will burst.

And then we'll emerge, in awful ranks,
a skull on our skulls and bony shanks;
and we'll roar in the faces of all the people
We, the dead, accuse!

### Alien Grave

A leaning cross and a cracked helmet;
the rain will not water the parched earth.
In that tomb beneath the collapsed tower
like aliens in an alien grave lie
Europe's slaughtered youth.

Cluttered up with a rickety birchwood cross
that grave becomes a dreadful sore.
And alien here, in a distant alien land
among the bones, are the ideals
of twenty youthful years

No, no monument is needed
on the grave in that silence
nor above them all a cross of metal.
That grave roars forth again and again
its eternal threnody

But when the storm blows over
who will understand, who will understand
that here in an alien grave there rots
(who will say for whose utopia)
Europe's betrayed youth?

### I Would Sooner Perish

I know: there are grand words
for which one may die.
Those words enkindle
and calm is cowardice
when they call out to the throng
beneath regimental colours.

But whoever knows the old mothers
left on their own
and the children without fathers
believes nothing they say.

I know: there are great deeds
and they require sacrifices.
I know: there are heroic deeds
used to hallow
the gains of purposeless wars
in lengthy truces.

But whoever saw from afar
ruined cathedrals
and smashed cities aflame
will not believe them any more.

I know: there are great men
with claims to immortality.
They have inscribed themselves upon the ages with their blood;
and there are more than enough of them
in the cemeteries of every land
in the shade of honourable linden trees.

But whoever has seen
beneath the bloodied sword
the wounded writhe in agony,
knows them even better.

I know: I am a small, wretched
and possibly despicable runt.
I know: these words of mine
are a dangerous poison
that can envenom
your high-flown song.

And yet I would sooner perish
with your spittle on my face,
I'd sooner die a coward
than have blood on my hands.

*Translated from the Czech by Gerald Turner*

# 7

# Journey to the Satellite City of the Metropolis of Death

All of what I said before has been my observation of myself. More precisely, it was reflective observation of my surroundings at the time and of what occurred in them, of selected critical episodes, but viewed through the prism of the landscapes of the Metropolis of Death.

Now I have to muster the courage to embark on a journey to realms that seemingly lie on its far side. A journey that will touch a living, searing point, shrouded under a light-and-shadow layer of obscure dimness, silent always. Here, too, it is possible to focus on describing individual scenes.

## At the Brink of the Exit from Hades

The first of them takes place in the heart of the Metropolis, but on the other side of the railway track and its last stop – the 'ramp' between the two crematoria structures I and II. The first scene, then, unfolds on the far side of the track, in the women's camp (*Frauenlager*) of Birkenau, in July 1944. This might be the beginning. The end or the continuation and the finality came long after, in a place quite distant, and is mysteriously connected to a powerful current of water; the current of time that passes the Metropolis of Death and, far from it, in one of its satellite cities, spills into the Baltic Sea. That end-journey – to Danzig and to the former Stutthof concentration camp – was made forty-eight years later, in October 1992, and is documented in my diary, covering the period from approximately October 1992 to February 1993.

21.

I return to July 1944: the last image, in fact the only one, of the parting from my mother. It was a few days after the final liquidation of the family camp, BIIb – that is, the liquidation of those who remained in it after the last, final selections. I, together with the group of youths, had been moved to the men's camp, BIId, while my mother, as I said, was moved to the other side into the grey-brick buildings of the women's camp.

There I met her for the last time, when I came to part from her. To see each other one more time, before her departure. I knew she was going to leave. For where? I did not know. This was before the leaving on that track which seemed to run in only one direction and to be swallowed up in the crematoria, or in that ramified net of spider's webs – the grid of camps – as we saw them when we arrived.

In my mind's eye I see images: one image. These are actually seconds, only seconds, seconds of a hasty farewell after which my mother turned around and started to walk into the distance toward those grey structures of the camp. She wore a thin skirt that rippled in the light breeze and I watched as she walked and receded into the distance. I expected her to turn her head, expected a sign of some kind. She did not turn her head but walked, walked until she became a speck at the other end, a speck I knew was that light summer skirt – and disappeared. I do not know how long I stood there. I could not understand. I went on wondering about the meaning of this riddle, the hard-heartedness of the act, followed by that slow vanishing which turned into a mere speck of colour. I thought about it afterwards, and think about it to this day: why did she not turn her head, at least once? I knew she was designated to go from that place – in that going, in that despairing attempt to go from the Auschwitz Hades. I do not know if I thought of it then, but whenever I reflect on that act, on those last minutes, it is impossible not to recall that archetypal myth of the attempt to get out of Hades. Who was Orpheus there and who Eurydice – that is not clear to me – but my mother did not turn her head, and went from that place and disappeared.

My simple explanation at the time was that if she had turned her head she would not have been able to endure the madness of the horror, the unbearable pain and the knowledge that she was leaving us there, my father and me, within the immutable law from which no one is exempt, certainly not me at the age I was then. And perhaps she feared that, amid this madness of pain, of returning to me, to us, we would all perish.

It was not until long afterwards, long after the war, long after the news of her death reached us, that I learned more, here in Jerusalem, from her companion in her last moments, or actually during the entire journey of leaving Auschwitz and during the time of that satellite city of the Metropolis of Death, Stutthof camp; learned something that offered a different interpretation, perhaps, for the impenetrable mystery of that determined walking away and that disappearance into the way out of there: my mother was carrying the embryo of my brother, an Auschwitz embryo, from her meeting with father there, and also her resolve to try to leave at least with him, if we two were to remain and perish.

She bore all the ordeals of the journey, the backbreaking work, and miraculously, and because of the skill and sacrifice of her women friends, she arrived at the hour of birth. The boy was born in Stutthof, and her friends, or the women who worked in the hospital, promised to preserve the newborn if no emergency arose and if no one entered from the ruling establishment, namely SS men. The infant was healthy and screamed like a healthy infant, and SS men who were about to approach brought about his end: those same women friends terminated his life. That great immutability of death, that Great Death which prevailed in Auschwitz – in which a crack seemed to have opened, of the railway track receding into the distance and the cars that carried the remnants of our camp, among them my mother, like a crack of hope to survive, to breach the wall of the immutable law – that unrelenting immutability was at work also far from the Metropolis: in that branch of the Great Death, in that satellite city, in Stutthof concentration camp, in the far north, on the shore of the Baltic Sea, at the estuary of the River Vistula; the river which, like the railway line, ran unhurriedly from the outskirts of Auschwitz into the vast and terrible forest which now stretches across the ground of that camp for Jewish women, as I saw it on the journey of the search for my mother's place of burial.

My mother recovered from the delivery before the evacuation of Stutthof camp. The death march was cruel in the extreme, the still surviving women subjected to horrific and brutal killing at the hands of the SS troops. She fled from that. She and her three friends fled shortly before the evacuation started and found shelter under assumed identities as German refugees from the nearby city of Elbing, which had been bombed, in a hut in the yard of a German farmer. There one

22.   23.

of the women fell ill, the woman who afterwards brought me the information about what befell my mother from the time she left Auschwitz until her last moments. My mother had in her possession a diamond which she had received from my father before she set out, to be used to look after herself and the baby when needed. She exchanged it for money, clothes and medicines and looked after the young woman who had fallen ill with the serious, usually fatal, disease of typhoid fever, which she had brought with her from Stutthof when they fled. She recovered. Afterwards, as she related in the visit to Jerusalem, my mother fell ill and did not recover. She is buried in that small village by the estuary of the River Vistula where the four found shelter, known then by its German name, Nickelswalde, and today by its Polish name, Mikoszewo, next to the German Protestant cemetery of that period. Nowadays it contains only a few graves of Polish Catholics, a place which, miraculously, we were able to locate.

24.

The immutable law of the Great Death, the immutable law which recurs in that dream in infinite permutations, which in one place I called 'the eternal death of the child', that terrible immutability did not cease even here, in the attempt to save her. Her last moments, her last hallucinations, as described by that friend of hers, were devoted to me: worry and nightmares in which she saw me hiding in a secret place which my father and I had prepared for the time when the

Czech camp, the family camp, would be liquidated, in the event that we would not leave it; that is, I would not be able to leave, I would not be included in the group of youths chosen for a further extension of life. Even though my mother knew I had got out, because when we last met I was already in a different part of the camp, the picture that stayed with her in those last nightmarish hours was of how I remained in that hiding place in the desolate camp; a hiding place which was in a kind of loft of the huge water tank in the inmates' large washing barracks, the barracks with the wonderful acoustics in which we sang – two hundred metres from the selections platform, about three hundred metres from the crematoria – where we sang then in the children's choir, conducted by the choirmaster, the 'Ode to Joy': 'Joy! Bright spark of divinity! ... Fire-inspired, we tread thy sanctuary.' Here the circle was closed, after I heard the conclusion of this tragedy, foreordained as it was, here, in Jerusalem of 1961.

## At the Estuary of the Great River of Time on the Shores of the Baltic Sea

I have related this story ahead of another end-story, in which an additional circle was closed: the story of the journey which my father and I took when we went to Danzig and to Stutthof. We went to look for the grave, to look for the satellite city of the Metropolis of Death – and we reached it. The gate, unlike the one in Birkenau, was well kept, and the buildings which greeted the visitors were as well guarded as they were preserved, with museum rooms and research rooms for the staff of the place, which had in the meantime become a memorial site. A memorial site mainly for the camp of the prisoners of the Polish national resistance movement against the Nazis. The avenue leading into the camp and its continuation inside recalled the well-kept camps, like Dachau in Germany, with floor plans, maps and statistical data, followed by a few rooms containing appurtenances of torture and devices for executions. But the camp itself, Stutthof itself, was a kind of field, a seemingly almost endless space, desolate yet somehow cultivated, the grass cut, a sort of lawn stretching – not endlessly, but to the edge of a large, black forest, beyond which was, we were told, the sea.

25.

As we stood there, in the late-October cold of the Baltic Sea, next to one of the floor plans of the well-kept camp, I broke away from the group and started to walk toward the forest. Because there, in that forest, as had been explained to us, had stood the camp of the Jewish women from Auschwitz. There, too, had been the large pit in which the bodies were burned.

I walked – I did not really know where I was going or what I wanted – I walked through the large space of the lawn, with no fences, no barbed wire, no high grass, no trees, through the space in which the camps were marked by roughly rectangular white structures made of hewn stone, with plaques on them denoting the individual camps that had been there in the past. I proceeded from one sort of monument to another, from one camp to the next, moving toward the forest where no structure stood and no stone lay. It was a place of primeval bleakness: marshes, fallen trees, white birches, dark trees and trees I did not bother to identify.

26.

I drew closer and after a certain hesitation I entered the forest.
I skirted the marshes, the puddles, and stopped where I stopped.

27.

I recited Kaddish, I read Kaddish, the Jewish prayer for the dead.
I started back.

28.

## *Strips of Leather*

Walking there, I saw ahead of me only the forest. Returning, my eyes were fixed on the ground. And as I scour the grass like this, aimlessly, almost every few steps I encounter strips of leather – dark, some rotted, dried out. I picked up one or two of them without knowing what I was doing, but, as in the return to Birkenau, when I picked up the fragment of a brick from the remnants of the youth and children's barracks and another fragment of brick from the rubble of the crematoria and took them with me to Jerusalem, this is undoubtedly what I wanted to do, and did, with these strips of leather. Because they were the only distinctive thing in that grass.

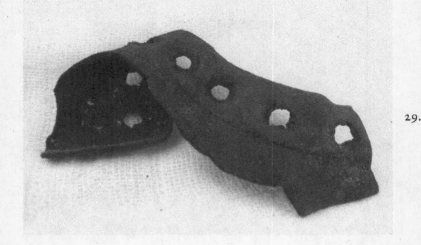

29.

I then returned and rejoined the accompanying group. We all went up to the well-kept, warm headquarters of the SS, now a place of research. The director of the site asked me, as a 'notable historian', to meet with the research staff and to partake of tea and biscuits. The occasion was difficult for me, but I tried to exchange a few words with them about matters of research. We were also given a photocopy from the card index of the female inmates, my mother's card, with her details: cause of death – blank; date of death – blank; date of arrival and former place of stay – Auschwitz. The card is in my possession to this day.

## 'What, here too . . . ?'

But the main reason I am describing this encounter is an event that came later, when we went to see the small exhibition displayed in the building. One of the items in it was a large, long glass case containing

30.

thousands of shoes, all in a jumble as they had been stuffed into the case, like one sees in photographs from the museum at Auschwitz.

We asked them, 'What, here too ... the women went to their death

31.

with their shoes taken from them beforehand?' For in Auschwitz those shoes belonged to hundreds of thousands of people who no longer needed them after taking them off in the corridors of the gas chambers. The director of the site said, 'No, these are shoes from Auschwitz.'

Indeed, just as Auschwitz sent the armies of slaves – the women – trainloads of slaves with heads shaved – it also sent freight cars of shoes, and the inmates of Stutthof were engaged in fixing and repairing and examining the shoes, in case hidden in them were the last treasures of those who perished.

From this industry, which afterwards sent the shoes to all parts of the Reich, there remained the strips of leather that were strewn across the whole vast area of the camps, which, as I noted, were cultivated so impressively in the form of a huge lawn and rectangular monuments made of white stone. Here, then, was another surprising connection between the Auschwitz Metropolis and its satellite city of Stutthof: not only were people caught up in the immutable law, notwithstanding that they had left that place, but the shoes of the murdered, of those who perished, accompanied them here. And this powerful current of the River Vistula, 'the wicked Vistula', the river

32.

whose upper stretch we had begun to approach back then, on my previous return to Auschwitz with the prattling driver from Kraków, who told about the wicked Vistula which overflowed its banks and harmed people and animals, and into which the ashes of the cremated were thrown – that is, into its tributary, the Sola, which empties into it: this Vistula, which crosses Poland from south to north, to the plains of East Prussia, and spills as a kind of vast delta into the Baltic Sea, symbolized that link, the link to the immutable law from which there is no escape.

## *It was on the Twenty-Fifth of January 1945*

So, too, there was no escaping it in the last place we came to. This was the village of Mikoszewo, lying at the end of the narrow railway line extending to the ferry that transported passengers across the great estuary. At that time, it was used to transport the prisoners who had survived the death march to the other side, to continue their journey.

33.

34.

That place became the site of the brutal massacre of all those who remained, my mother by then no longer among them. It lay a few dozen, a few hundred metres from the house in which she and her friends found shelter under assumed identities when they escaped, and, as I said, it was in that same place, close to that same Vistula, that we later found the cemetery. We found it on the basis of the testimony of the only German woman who was still alive from the German population of that time, and her grandfather, she told us, had also been the undertaker there. She remembered the coffins of two of the four women that were brought from that German farm for burial at night, one after the other. She pointed out the place. There were no headstones. Afterwards we returned from that place – first to Danzig, then to Prague, then to Jerusalem.

My diary entries for that journey contain highly detailed descriptions of the landscapes, the events, and also of my thoughts. What they do not contain is the start of the journey, the picture of the start, the parting at Auschwitz, that desperate attempt to get out of Hades and the story of the new life which had supposedly eluded the fate that governed everyone, even far from there. In that foredoomed tragedy, for which I evoked the Orphean myth, it was impossible to cross the River Styx of the Vistula back to life. It was possible only to set forth on it and flow north with its current. And as the unfolding of the immutable law overtook even the small death – even the small being – through the hands of the self-righteous hospital women, perhaps messengers of fate, the Great Death overtook my mother, too, there. It was on the twenty-fifth of January 1945, not long before the village was liberated – or conquered, as the local German population felt it then – by the Soviet army.

35.

# 8

# Landscapes of a Private Mythology

*At the Sealed Gate of Mercy*

In this chapter I move to a very different time, to Jerusalem of the late 1960s. I do not remember if it was immediately after the war – the Six Day War – or some time later, after I returned from a year in England, but the place where I underwent this experience was the Temple Mount. It was my first visit to the Temple Mount, or at least to its desolate and neglected north-eastern part, past the Dome of the Rock on the way to the Gate of Mercy, the sealed Golden Gate.[1]

36.

I went alone. I crossed the tiled plaza, passed by the ancient magnificence which had survived. I continued to the untended, desolate area, which was entirely overgrown with grass and high thorns – not so high, but dense, dark, grey – and an overwhelming quiet accompanied me as I approached the descent to the blocked gate.

Suddenly I was struck by a feeling of absolute certainty, not to be questioned: *in this place I have been before!*

That was absurd, of course. Of course I had not been to this place, not ever, could not have been, but the certainty was total, unmistakable. I wrack my brain, try to analyse things, identify details, probe feelings, find explanations – and at that moment I stopped. Stopped next to rusting barbed wire that had been thrown into the grass which grew wildly there. The identification seems very simple, though one could ask: 'What is the connection between barbed wire here and Auschwitz?' It was clear to me that this was not Auschwitz of its 'period of glory and grandeur', but Auschwitz of that first dim visit from the years after the war, which had apparently sunk completely into my memory and which I have not mentioned until now. The visit of a fourteen-year-old boy, in order to appear as a witness in a trial held in Kraków in 1946 against Auschwitz criminals. While there, we were permitted to visit Auschwitz itself, and we also reached Birkenau.

37.

The primal experience of those desolate ruins, of that terrible contrast, of a place charged with historic meaning, an event on a colossal scale, dramatic, teeming with people, death, history; the consciousness of such highly charged meaning now apparelled as a ruin, and the contrast between this and the sense one had then of vast events unfolding being so grating yet so pertinent – here, apparently, lay the root cause of the amazement which struck the tourist walking on the Temple Mount and cut through the layers sealed by the passage of time.

Indeed, that place was charged like no other with the unfolding of a historical trauma, with death and end-time, with everything that came out of it or flowed into it, and walking across it was to make one's way through the mute ruins, through grass growing wild, amid the rusting barbed wire that links this place to that. Had it not been for that barbed wire, there might never have arisen that stunning and unmistakable feeling: *in this place I have been before!*

When I understood this I returned to Auschwitz. Not immediately. I left the Temple Mount, physically, but in my consciousness returned to Auschwitz. It must have been then that I arrived at the decision to return there and wander through that desolation, amid the polarity in which of course I always feel the heaving presence of life and death there, the machinery of that fearful history which is no more. This is what always draws me back to that fearful immutable law which seizes me and does not release me and whose essence has, for me, remained there. It was apparently then that I decided, perhaps without being aware of it, to return. That is the background for what happened ten years later, in the journey to Poland in 1978, when I took part in a scientific conference whose end was the return journey to the Metropolis of Death – as perhaps it still is today. I do not think I will go back to that place again, but that visit, which I made alone, probably had its genesis in my astonishing experience then, on the desolate and neglected Temple Mount, opposite the sealed Gate of Mercy.[2]

# 38

# The Blue Skies of Summer

Another leap in time, to a different landscape and different colours. The colour is blue: clear blue skies of summer. Silver-coloured toy aeroplanes carrying greetings from distant worlds pass slowly across the azure skies while around them explode what look like white bubbles. The aeroplanes pass by and the skies remain blue and lovely, and far off, far off on that clear summer day, distant blue hills as though not of this world make their presence felt. That was the Auschwitz of that eleven-year-old boy. And when this boy, the one who is now recording this, asks himself – and he asks himself many times – what the most beautiful experience in your childhood landscapes was, where you escape to in pursuit of the beauty and the innocence of your childhood landscapes, the answer is: to those blue skies and silver aeroplanes, those toys, and the quiet and tranquillity that seemed to exist all around; because I took in nothing but that beauty and those colours, and so they have remained imprinted in my memory.

This contrast is an integral element of the black columns that are swallowed up in the crematoria, the barbed-wire fences that are

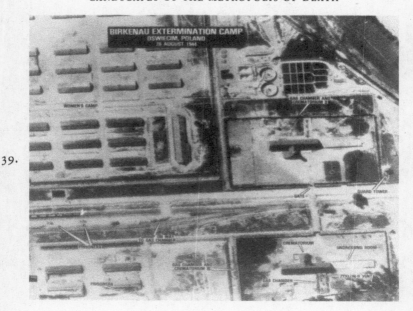

39.

stretched tight all around by the concrete pillars. But in that experience all this seemingly did not exist, only in the background and not consciously.

Consciousness has internalized and submerged the sensation of the bold summer colours of that immense space; of the cerulean skies, the aeroplanes – and of the boy gazing at them and forgetting everything around him. There is almost no return to that Metropolis, with its sombre colours, with the sense of the immutable law that encloses all its beings within confines of allotted time and of death; that is, there is almost no sense of a return to that world without a sense of return to those wonderful colours, to that tranquil, magical and beckoning experience of those blue skies of the summer of 1944 in Auschwitz-Birkenau.

I can search for a great many similar experiences, perhaps from before Auschwitz was, from before the expulsion was, in my earlier childhood: landscapes of childhood in Bohemia, green and bright – but they all pale. So too with later landscapes in Israel, landscapes in fiery colours under a blazing light of yellow and blue – the blue of the sky in this land is many times stronger than any blue one can see anywhere else, or that I have seen elsewhere. But even so, the one is pale and blurred, the other strong and harsh and somehow does not belong. The only belonging blue, overcoming every other colour, imprinted in my memory as the colour of summer, the colour of tranquillity, the colour of forgetting – momentary forgetting – is that colour of a Polish summer in 1944. And for that little boy who is part of that summer, all this will remain for all time as a touchstone of beauty, nonpareil in all the landscapes I have collected into myself and which I will probably be able to collect – how to put it, in a phrase – for all time. I do not know how much longer I have until that 'for all time', but I have absolutely no doubt that to here I will always return. This return, even if it is divorced from that sombre return from which there is no way out, is itself a return which has no way out. The colour is the colour of childhood, a colour of innocence, a colour of beauty. And this too is an immutable law from which there is no escape. There is no escape from beauty, from the sense of beauty at the height and in the midst of the Great Death which governs all.

# 9

## Rivers which Cannot be Crossed and the 'Gate of the Law'

These images of skies of blue and columns of people in black being swallowed into the confines of the crematoria and disappearing in clouds of smoke, the corridors of lights leading to the Metropolis of Death, the terms 'Metropolis of Death' and 'Homeland of Death', all of which are so close to me; landscapes to which I escape as one escaping into the landscapes of childhood, feeling in them a sense of freedom, protected by that immutable law of the all-pervasive dominion of death, by the beauty of summer landscapes – all these things are part of a private mythology which I am conscious of, a mythology that I forged, that I created, with which I amuse myself and in which – I will not even say I am tormented, I am not tormented – I find an escape when other things haunt me, and even when they don't. This Homeland exists and is available to me always. But it is a myth, it has its own mythological language, and what I am doing here actually runs contrary to all my decisions, all my feelings, the whole awareness of my limitations, or former limitations that came to mind: limitations of language, primarily doubts of my ability to intermix these mythological landscapes with landscapes that are receptive to communicative transmission. These doubts, or the avoidance of involving these landscapes in any other aspect of my everyday life, and also rising above or making an intellectual effort to understand the world and explain it, which I do to the best of my ability almost daily as a teacher in one of our respected academic institutions, one of whose aims is to confer interpretation and meaning on human existence in the past and in the near past – my area of specialization – all these things, along with this separation, this avoidance of mixing one sphere with another, stemmed from an unshakable determination and were my guiding light.

Thus, until now only the pages of my diary shared with me the trips to that mythic Homeland, to that Metropolis. I won't say that I didn't try to share – not actively but passively, like any thinking person anywhere – I won't say that I avoided entirely trying to share in others' attempts to evoke those landscapes, or those seeming landscapes, by others who considered this a mission and did meaningful things and transmitted the message. Here and there I tried, by which I mean – let me put it the other way around – I in fact refrained, and continue to refrain to this day, from reading anything literary or artistic that describes or tries to describe Auschwitz, the concentration camps, this chapter of the 'Final Solution' or the history of the Jews within its unfolding, namely the violent end. I have similarly refrained from visiting exhibitions or museums, and however much time I spend in various archives and libraries, including the Yad Vashem Archives and the Yad Vashem library, I have not visited, and probably will not visit – will not be capable of visiting – either the exhibition or this great memorial site of Yad Vashem or other such exhibitions and memorials. I have not seen the film *Shoah*, which so many have made part of their intellectual or experiential property. Why I avoided seeing the film and always put it off and in the end did not see it, was not always clear to me. Nor do I see other films on these subjects and never gave myself an accounting as to why. It is certainly not, as the usual interpretation might have it, because it would cause me suffering or make me flinch. Of course not. But my stance of remoteness, which I developed in dealing with the history of this period, perhaps obliged me to avoid over-involvement in regard to that final violent stage.

That was what I thought for a long time, though without ever actually giving myself a convincing explanation. But there *is* a convincing explanation. I arrived at it about three years ago, and I think it also exists in one of the diary entries, maybe from 1989. However, even if it is not recorded there, or is formulated differently from the way I see it today, I want to conclude this chapter with an attempt to clarify, to interpret things as they came to me in a moment of enlightenment – the light by which I live in these mythic landscapes of my private mythology, these home landscapes of Auschwitz, the Homeland of Death, the Metropolis, and all the rest.

It began with the following episode: a university colleague invited me to attend a lecture on the subject of the Holocaust in literature. Common courtesy forbade me to decline the invitation, and I heard what I heard. The feeling of alienation was overwhelming. These are two different languages: one language which I do not understand, and a second language through which I live that period. Nevertheless, I went ahead and read one of the books that were mentioned in the lecture. After all, some of the books were written by people here whom I know – excellent writers, who are frequently quoted – and there are excellent writers elsewhere who have obviously confronted the subject and deserve to be subjects of research and analysis. I took one of these books, perhaps one of the finest of them, and started to read – about Auschwitz: a description of a situation the author experienced. To my appalled astonishment, all I felt, all I read and saw in that evocation, in those descriptions, was utter alienation. Between the description of a world, the description of landscapes, the description of a reality which was divorced from the images, the scenes, the landscapes, the experiences, the presence of the past that is perpetually part of my present, there are rivers that cannot be crossed. In no way can I connect and integrate these things into those landscapes.

Here I asked this naive question: after all, for the whole world, or for the whole reading public everywhere, that book and many others like it, and many works of cinema, theatre and art, offer a way to understand and experience Auschwitz, its universe, the ghettos, that final stage, that reality. And everyone reads these books – they sell thousands of copies – so they obviously speak in a uniform language to all those myriad readers. *Yet I cannot find in them what they seek to convey!* It's a completely different world! The only response I feel able to express is alienation; all that is authentic is the authenticity of the alienation. Therefore I ask: *in what am I different? Something is wrong with me!*

And then, as so often, as almost always during periods of distress, I escape to Kafka, either his diaries or his other works. At that time, I again opened at the ending – I always open randomly – I opened at the ending of the wonderful story of the man standing before the Gate of the Law. This man who stands before the Gate of the Law actually asks the same question – and it is one of the last questions he asks, driven by his insatiable curiosity, as the gatekeeper jests. He asks: 'Tell me, after all this is the Gate of the Law, and the Gate of the Law is open to everyone.' To which the gatekeeper says: 'Yes, that is so.' Then the man says (if I remember the text correctly): 'Yet in all the years I have been sitting here no one has entered the gate.' And the gatekeeper nods his head and says: 'Indeed.' The man asks him to explain this puzzling fact, and the gatekeeper does him this one last mercy and says: 'This gate is open only for you, it exists only for you, and now I am going to close it.'

Accordingly, everything I have recorded here – all these landscapes, this whole private mythology, this Metropolis, Auschwitz – this Auschwitz that was recorded here, which speaks here from my words, is the only entrance and exit – an exit, perhaps, or a closing – the only one that exists for me alone. I take this to mean that I cannot enter by any other way, by any other gate to that place. Will others be able to enter through the gate that I opened here, that remains open for me? It is possible that they will, because this gate that Kafka opened, which was intended for only one person, for K., Josef K., is actually open to almost everyone. But for him there was only one gate into his private mythology.

I don't know whether this analogy is valid here, but this is the only meaning I can find for the puzzle of the occupation of my present with that past, which I experience constantly, in which I create constantly, to which I escape constantly, in which I create landscapes intermixed with scenes of childhood reality and time and of the onlooker, of the big boy looking with puzzlement at all this, and who, before it is shut – before that gate is shut – asks these questions and, at least to this mystifying matter, seems to have found an answer at last. It's not much, a marginal thing, really, but it is impossible not to convey these things, not to puzzle over them, not to believe in them, for without that belief the whole memory of my childhood landscapes, the landscapes in which I always find freedom – my last but one freedom – would be lost.

# 10

# In Search of History and Memory

All this relates to the question of why I was incapable of viewing or reading works about the Holocaust. Yet was this really true, or was it only seemingly so? My direct confrontation with the world of the Metropolis, with the immutable law of the Great Death, occurred also in another channel, which from several points of view can be said to be the central channel of my life's work: scientific historical research. Indeed, I have already noted the paradoxical duality of my study of that period, with its systematic, total avoidance of integrating any detail of biographical involvement into the arena of the events of that history; indeed, into the very heart of those historical events.

I have dwelt on the duality, the methodological distancing, and all the rest. Yet the truth, as it seems to me now, is that I only tried to bypass here the barrier of that gate, to enter it with the whole force of my being, in the guise of, or in the metamorphosis of, perhaps, a Trojan horse, intended, finally, to smash the gate and shatter the invisible wall of the city forbidden to me, outside whose domain I had decreed that I would remain. For that rigorous 'pure scientific' writing is fraught with tremendous 'meta-dimensional' baggage and tensions, which are somehow time-transcendent.

Here, in this safe and well-paved way of scientific discipline, I believed that I would be able to infuse a consciousness of the intensity of the experience of those historic events, a consciousness of their trans-dimensionality, a consciousness of their vast impersonality, which I experienced through the prism of that present – its memory and its imagining, from which I flinched and which I feared, perhaps subconsciously, to confront head-on.

The fact is that in all my research I never had to deal with the stage, the dimension, of the violent end, the murder, the humiliation and the torture of those human beings. I left, or skirted that dimension – as perhaps I skirted the piles of skeletons of the corpses that were heaped up behind the barracks in Auschwitz on my way to the youth hut – in order to study the broad background of the ideology and the policy underlying it all, the historical implications, the dynamics of society and government, and the society and leadership of those who were the objects of the 'Final Solution' – the Jews – in the period preceding that stage of a violent, ultimate end. I hoped, apparently, that in this way I would be able to cope with the sense of 'mission' of the bearer of the message, the knowledge, that were burned into my being, and had I not found that 'safe passage' I could not have borne those tensions and anxieties, when I stood helpless, cowering at the vague awareness that I had no way, and would never attempt, to embark on the path of an attempt to disclose that message and all it contains: that the world, with the Metropolis and the immutable law of the Great Death having been, can no longer and will never again be able to free itself of their being part of its existence.

Was that my gate to the law? To the law of the world? One of the two massive iron doors of that gate, a gate that is open day and night? And now, as the gatekeeper said to the man, 'I am going to close it.' Yet it seems to me that story also tells, that in those moments it appeared to the man that beyond that gate there shone, or glowed dimly, a new light, such as he had never before seen in his life.

40.

# Three Chapters from
the Diaries

# Dream: Jewish Prague and the
# Great Death

*Diary entry, 28 July 2003*

A deserted street in Prague, in the ancient Jewish Quarter. I am sitting
in a car of faded colour, blocked in a crowded parking area. But
'crowded' here means three or four nondescript cars, which blend
into the surrounding bleakness. The time – the bleak time of the
dominion of the immutable Great Death. From envoys of the Jewish
Town Hall I receive – hesitantly – a message announcing a verdict: I
am to proceed to the Jewish Town Hall, the building with the baroque
tower and the clocks with Hebrew and Roman numerals, located not
far from there on the same way, closed and locked and deserted-
looking from the outside.

From the moment this verdict – why do I use this term? That is
how I dreamed it, and its linguistic origin in my head is immaterial at
present – the moment I receive this order I set out on my way, which
will not end until the end of the dream and not until today, until this
hour and not in all the hours that follow this one.

But how can I set out when parked close behind me is a dusty car
like mine, which seems to have been here a long time, while in front
of me is a grey-black truck – its colour is indistinct – not especially
large but blocking my way out.

There are few pedestrians on the empty street, and no traffic. It is
a sombre, piercing winter day – it is not snowing but winter's terror
pervades all. If there are people in this city, on this street, they are shut
up in their homes. Here and there a few people skitter by, indifferent,
withdrawn, like shadows of the dead, hurrying about their business.

The picture that arose in my mind then, based on the photographs
and documents of that period in the history of Prague Jewry – during
and after the mass deportations – was of those few who remained and

41.

were put to work cataloguing, recording and storing 'the treasures of the glorious Jewish past', a past which was frozen and thrust into deep-freeze then. Muted. And they, too, the few who were engaged in this, did not speak to me and did not reply to my questions – 'How do I get to . . .' – but hurried about their business. Like people from that order, who know its nature and know their place in it.[1] What exactly did I try to ask there, on that deserted street in the Jewish Quarter of Prague at that time, when I was handed the order and had not yet left the blocked parking place? I tried to ask the way, how to get to the Jewish Town Hall, even though it was only a few dozen metres away, on the same street, and I knew exactly what it looked like. Nevertheless, I had to ask how to get there, because even though the order, or the 'verdict', was unequivocal, getting there was neither simple nor unequivocal.

After some time – exactly how long is now difficult for me to estimate – the truck driver appeared and I tried to remonstrate with him feebly about the delay he had caused me, but he paid no attention, and if, a bit put out, he mumbled something, it was more to himself than a response to my remarks. The truck started up and left, and I was able to get out of the parking place. I did so – but more I do not remember about if and where I got to in the car. What I do remember well is that immediately afterwards I found myself walking on that same street and wanting to reach the destination mentioned in the order I had been given.

I knew exactly what was going on inside then, and for what purpose I had to go to that sombre building. It was obvious to me that what was going on inside was what went on in the structure that housed the gas chambers in Birkenau to which I was ordered to go, and went, and escaped, and was sent back, and so forth. And it all proceeds quietly, without a word being uttered by those serving in it like dark shadows by the flickering light of the fire in the furnaces.

I can no longer remember whether I went back and asked passers-by on the street – if there were any, and it seems to me that there were and that they remained indifferent to my questions, as before – but when I reached the Town Hall, the building's heavy iron door (in reality there are heavy wooden doors) was locked. I knocked on this iron gate, which is painted a light grey, faded perhaps, but got no response from within.

As I stood in front of this locked gate, expecting it to open – for, after all, I could not but enter it once the parking area was unblocked and I could supposedly move about on my own – the picture changed completely. The lowering winter day dissolved into the light of a clear summer day, the streets filled up with people, and I found myself making my way among the many people who were sitting in the city's street cafés and restaurants, and continuing to walk along until I

42.

reached the magnificent Příkopy Boulevard, which was bustling with people, but no one took any notice of me and I too had nothing to ask any of them. It was clear to everyone, and to me as well, from the light and the atmosphere in the street that the war was over and that that regime had gone for good. But it was even clearer to me that this had nothing to do with me and my existential situation, because I was still – or again – on the way there, to the Town Hall, and absolutely had to get there.

Then I see, sitting at a table in one of the cafés along the boulevard, Livia Rothkirchen, an old acquaintance of my father and of mine, a former employee of Yad Vashem, and an inhabitant of the landscapes of the Metropolis of Death at the time, beaming at me and calling to me happily, '*Pane Kulka, Pane Kulka, vždyť to už je všechno pryč!*' – 'Mr Kulka, Mr Kulka, all that has already passed and vanished, you know!' And I wonder and am astonished, or perhaps am not astonished but a little puzzled at what this has to do with the fact that I am still on the same street and must get to the same place, and that what is going on inside is proceeding according to that order. And it is also clear to me that in the end this iron gate will have to be opened for me. Only one detail, perhaps not very significant, but bothersome and persistent, remains unrelentingly unclear to me: does the implementation of the verdict I was given destine me – after I enter – for those ovens or for the traditional hanging device, which is situated in the Town Hall compound but outside the walls of the building itself, on some sort of balcony or upper courtyard on the roof of the jutting lower floor, on the side opposite the direction of the Altneuschul synagogue?

Thus I have reconstructed that dream occurrence – fragments upon fragments, in large segments one after the other, but always informed by wholeness and a clear certainty, and time, or the change of time, did not and could not possess any significance. What changed in it was only the setting, which shifted and moved between the Metropolis of Death – Auschwitz – and the Metropolis of the land of my birth – Prague.

# 12

# Doctor Mengele Frozen in Time

*Diary entry, 22 January 2001*

I had the dream the night before, but yesterday, from the morning and throughout the entire day, I had to finish writing a biographical survey about my father, in connection with a plan to install a bust of him in a public space in Prague. Now, in the small hours, I return to the dream as it arose and was preserved in my memory.

Well, on that night, in that dream, I was again in Auschwitz, in one of the crematoria. More accurately, in its ruins. I entered the dream through its ruins. They were the ruins of the crematorium I had not entered on my return journey but had stood opposite and observed the blackening remains from which shrubs and weeds sprouted.

43.

I do not know how I entered, or even how it was possible to enter, but I entered and was inside. There I saw a long chamber, a concrete structure that had not been destroyed, its ruined state solely the result of years of neglect. The structure was entirely above ground and lit by the light of day. There was also a very long table and benches made of rough boards. Sitting at the table was a group of visitors who were touring Auschwitz, all of them Israelis, not young, but probably none of them, it seemed to me, had experienced Auschwitz in those days, in its 'glory' period.

All of them were listening attentively to an explanatory talk by the site's guide about the structure and its functions and about the camp. And the guide, the explainer on behalf of the camp's present-day Polish directorate, was Doctor Mengele!

Everyone listened to his informative explanations without comment, but it was clear to them all and also to me that it was he, in his present function as explainer and guide at the site.

44.

45.

Externally he did not resemble the person I had known then or later photographs published in the press from somewhere in South America. This was a person in his fifties or sixties, with greying hair, quite a round face, and of average height; but as I noted, it was clear to me and to all the others that it was him. Doctor Mengele.

I spoke with him. His present job did not strike me as so odd, but what I did find odd and asked him about explicitly was, 'Where were you in all the years since then?' His reply, which seemed to him the most natural and self-evident in the world, was, 'What do you mean, where was I? I was here. I was here all the time.' That is, in this structure amid these ruins, in this peculiar structure about whose function there could also be no doubt, even though its form did not testify to that. But plainly, he had been there all along. And it was impossible, or there seemed to be no reason or cause, to doubt this. Perhaps he was like one of those timeless apparitions that inhabit mysterious old buildings or their ruins. But that is only a second thought, perhaps something that also underlay that 'self-evident' feeling, though when I spoke with him he was a normal human figure in every respect.

On the table there was a telephone, similar to the flat, grey phones in the teachers' rooms at the university. I remember that I phoned my late father to tell him that Mengele was there and that he could interview him. And I remember also that my father arrived, though I do not know if he interviewed him, if it came to that. However, I do remember very distinctly that one of the Israelis who was sitting at that long table and listening to the explanations, someone who had clearly not been in a camp, turned to me resentfully in astonished protest: 'How can you talk to him?' It was clear to us both that by 'him' he meant Doctor Mengele, not as a guide and explainer in his present function but in his identity then.

I, however, found nothing strange or unreasonable about this, from my point of view. Nor do I remember any longer whether I even tried to reply or explain.

This is what I remember, and it seems to me that I remember the essence, or everything.

I add no attempt at interpretation, even if there is much place for this.

# 13

# God's Grieving

*Diary entries, 17 August 2002 and
15 November 2002*

17.8.2002. A dream about undergoing God's physical existence or physical presence – in the crematorium; or a dream about God's existence and question of God's existence. It was not a question at all but an answer – in the dream, in Auschwitz, in the crematorium – a dream with a recurring setting: I entered it through the ruins of Crematorium No. II, on the right side of the railway line, the side facing 'our

46.

camp'. I wrote it down afterwards on scraps of paper, today, the day after the night of the dream: Shabbat morning, month of Av (I don't know the date of the Hebrew month), the seventeenth of August according to the gentile calendar.

15.11.2002.[1] Friday afternoon, Givat Ram campus. This beauty, this quiet, everything deserted outside, the sky still blue though not pristine. The mute buildings and the young trees, planted after the big snow – nothing moves or stirs in them. Silence and quiet expectation, tense perhaps, though with no outward sign, imprinted in everything. In every detail around and in what's between horizon and horizon. Expectation of what? Of winter's stormy winds and lightning flashes? Of an approaching disaster. Of the Great Death in its transmigration to this place, to this land and to this city – the 'Eternal City', the 'Promised Land' – the resurrection of the dominion of death – here?

There is no rainbow in the cloud.[2] In the Midrash it is written, 'I did not say by fire.'[3] The Great Death had – anteceding the fire – an exhalation of gas. 'What has been is what shall be,' said Kohelet, a king in Jerusalem[4] – the inhalation of gas, 'chemical and biological warfare' *haba aleinu letova*[5] – 'and shall we not accept the bad?'[6] – preceding the 'great fire', and 'not by the fire' of the Great Death, rather by the tremendous all-liquefying heat, then a 'slight voice of stillness'. This terrible silence and a street map of the great Kingdom of Death, black, scorched, mute – an aerial photograph of – of the gigantic footsteps of the Great Death which remained there. Like an aerial photograph from that time.[7] And the 'what shall be' has already been – here? And the young trees and the quiet: are they only the reflection of a remote past on remote stars?

I reflect a great deal on the grotesque dream I dreamed a few months ago here in Jerusalem, about 'Doctor Mengele and his incarnation in frozen time',[8] as though within an anachronistic bubble in contemporary garb: a 'guide for the unknowing' hired by the Auschwitz Museum to show visitors – some of them from Israel – around the remains of the camp. I entered those ghostly chambers then through the ruins of Crematorium No. II, on the 'other' side of the railway line, from which there was no way out other than this last stop.

'What do you mean, where was I? I was here. I was here all the time.' This abandoned industrial structure from a past time contained a hall adorned here and there with spider's webs, grimy windows, long uncleaned, across its entire length, and wooden tables and benches made from unfinished planks (like in our sawmill, with its large surfaces on which the boards for drying were stacked, like pyramids but without the hard stone tip that freezes over time beneath empty desert skies). My father was there, too: I called him on a telephone that stood on one of the tables, unthinkingly raising him up from Hades. He came, but I do not remember one word he uttered there, having come.

Yes, that weird dream occupies me again from time to time. Though only as a prelude, a corridor and a backdrop to another dream,[9] its variation – no, its transfiguration: into a dream about terrible grief, 'God's grieving', for He was there, then.

Human figures, like silhouettes from a shadow play, sway silently to and fro by the flickering light of the fire that burns in the ovens of that crematorium – not as an anachronistic spectacle like in the 'Mengele dream' but in Auschwitz real time, in its mute glory, against the backdrop of the darkly burning cremation ovens.

47.

Here is what I wrote on the scraps of paper on the day after the dream:

And I saw – the terrible grief of God, who was there. All that time. In His image. At first I felt Him (only) as a kind of mysterious radiation of pain, flowing at me from the dark void in the unlit part of the crema-tion ovens. A radiation of insupportably intense pain, sharp and dull alike. Afterwards He began to take the shape of a kind of huge embryo, shrunk with pain, in a murkiness amid which flickered only a little of the light cast by the raging fire locked in the heavy iron ovens. Shrunken like something, like someone whose large arms and fleshy body hover in Michelangelo's vast fresco on the ceiling of the Sistine Chapel, but in the form He took here He was alive, shrunken, hunched forward with searing pain, as in the twisted posture of Rodin's sculpture *The Thinker*. A figure on the scale of His creatures, in the form of a human being who came and was there – also – as one of His creatures in the kingdom of slave armies that were all around. And here too He did come and was in the dream, in this frightful incarnation which came into being (or appeared *deus ex machina, obscura, tremens*) as a response to 'the question they were forbidden to ask there' but was asked and floated in that dark air.

And from where in that dream did the question rise that brought forth His image and lit it sparingly, there, in those dismal spaces?
From here, possibly.
It happened like this; and not in a dream.
My father used to research and record – here in Israel, for the most part – the shadow figures that had then slid past the cremation ovens, in the harsh blazing light of this land. One of the questions or com-ments that recurred in his conversations with them – a variation on the numberless reproofs of those who, already there, severed their former universe of belief with a sharp knife – was: 'Is there indeed no God?' And, 'If there was, where was He then and how did He allow that which befell this generation to take place?' and similar variations of cogent truth and of its use, knowingly or unknowingly, in retro-spect, or at the time of 'that truth' and the time of the 'great lie' that followed, and to the present day.

This question was asked there by those in the *Sonderkommando*, they who asked, spoke and wrote at that time, and some of whose words that were interred in the soil of death beneath their feet are still alive.

My father asked this question persistently – asked them and others of his contemporaries, here, in the interviews he recorded. So it was in one of his last visits to Bikur Holim Hospital, at the corner of Strauss and Nevi'im Streets, when I was with him, having taken him there.

In the hospital room with him was a large man, large of body and large in the reverence shown him by the many followers and disciples who came to the bed of their rabbi there. My father, as was his way – without reverence – plied his roommate, the 'great rabbi', who was about his age or perhaps a little younger, with questions to get him to talk. This was the scene in my mind's eye when he asked him something to this effect: 'Where were you and your followers at that time, what did you do [here in the Land of Israel, as the man and his followers looked as though they were from nearby ultra-Orthodox *Me'ah She'arim*], what did you ask, if you asked, and how did you reply to the question, "Where was God?"'

This rabbi of sorrows, but still projecting power and authority and reverence, whom people revered (not my father), replied with unabashed reluctance. (My father spoke to him in German, which he may have thought was like Yiddish – finding, as always, a way to engage in dialogue in every language and every situation.) 'Yes, we were here. Yes, at that time. But that question', as he also told his followers there, 'is one that it is forbidden to ask.' (Forbidden to be uttered, I put it to myself; forbidden to be raised then, or now and – here I add my own interpretation – 'for all eternity'.) Indeed, so it was there (in the hospital), and I was there.

But this, after all, is how it was there, too, in the darkness heaving through the fire's light, the shadow figures that slid by and left writings that I read, and my father, too, asked and recorded those who emerged from there, into the harsh blazing light of this land.

This is what he told me, in his apartment in the Kiryat Yovel neighbourhood of Jerusalem, in his study crammed with books, with folders holding the transcripts of the recordings he made, and numberless tapes that he recorded, all now located in the archives that are in the cellars under the Hill of Remembrance at Yad Vashem:

> The *Sonderkommandos* had a Jewish Kapo, or perhaps not a Kapo but a large man bearing the authority of one learned in the Torah, whom everyone regarded as a master and a leader and a rock of security. [I imagined him as a dark figure, big-bodied, a 'rock of security', mostly silent and taciturn, but replying to the questions of his venerators and co-sojourners in the darkness and the light from the fire of the cremation ovens.]
>
> They asked him those questions, too, and that question, then, in the real time of the Metropolis of Death in its 'glory' – 'Where is God?' – and the other variations on that question which was asked there, in that place of truth.
>
> And the rabbi – the Kapo – the teacher – the authority, the rock of their security amid the dark of that fire, replied – so they replied to my father: 'It is forbidden to ask that question, those questions, there, and unto eternity.'

Here I return to the last dream, which I jotted down on scraps of paper:

Indeed, it was forbidden to ask, there (and unto eternity). For He was, was present, there, too.

I conjured up more in that pre-dawn dream, or replied to questions and reflections which I had pursued already in wakefulness, invoking, actualizing and finally imprinting the images of that dream in my living memory:

Was it not like that, after all, with the terrible suffering of Job, when He (blessed be He) placed him in the hands of His dark faithful servant. For he was the one who said and did and the Kingdom of Evil came into being, as powerful as 'the immutable law of the Great Death' (in my words); 'Margrave of Gomorrah,' Gerschon wrote, and Dan Pagis wrote about this writing (of Gerschon) upon being informed by me of Gerschon's death, helpless in the face of his futile attempts to 'translate' Gerschon's poems into the language of Scripture.[10]

They both wrote about Cain and about Abel, [11] while I, in my own way, research the ways and the world and the 'self-understanding' of 'the great Cain'.

Thus did the emissary of 'He who spoke and brought the world into being' act and rule, and He spoke and allowed all this – all this, too – in the world of those created in His image, and He was grieved and was with them, and felt Job's pain when he 'was in the hand' of His great, dark servant. For what He spoke and allowed to come into being – the 'immutable law of the Great Death and its dominion' as it was then, over against which we sang in that Metropolis of Death, to which I returned, and return again, in dream and in reverie, in infinite variations – did exist and was not just a parable.[12]

In this immutable law which He set in motion as the 'unmotivated motivator', with this immutable law which, like all things, He spoke and it was, His hands were bound in speaking to His dark 'faithful

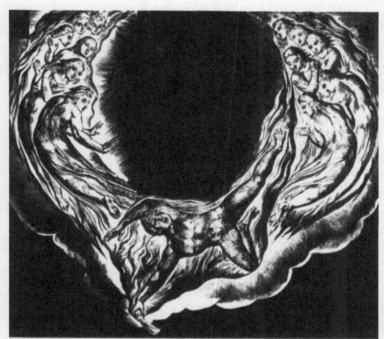

48.

Then went Satan forth from the presence of the Lord
And it grieved him at his heart
Who maketh his Angels Spirits & his Ministers a Flaming Fire

servant', in all his incarnations, in all generations, as it is written: 'Behold, he is in your hand, but preserve his life.' 'Then went he forth from the presence of the Lord.'[13]

And I, am I part of the remnants of the atoms of the eternal Job, one whose life was not taken? (Thus in the version I etched in my memory – but it is undeniably true.) And likewise that big, grim-faced rabbi who so reluctantly answered my father in the hospital, for he too was one of the souls, remnants of those whose lives were not taken but preserved by the dictum of Law of the Great Decisor who spoke and it was. The world was. And His creations. The great Cain, too, whom He created and into whose hand he gave Abel for all his generations. My beloved Dan Pagis: do you hear this, there, in the Hades on high?

Of all this, what was the dream, what were my dark reflections? But that which I dreamed I cannot but experience again in my memory: as the memory of the incarnations of the immutable law of the Great Death – the Markgraf of the Metropolis of Death.

There I saw with my own senses Him who spoke and the world was, and there was also him and his dominion, and there was Cain, and there was the insupportable grief which He in His own guise suffered and He shrank and whose radiance in that dark I too beheld, in that dream, in the real time which then was, and in my present time and in His, in the realms of the Metropolis of Death.

It is almost seven, Shabbat is already entering and I must go to usher in Shabbat with the children of the sons and daughters of Job the Just.

And Cain hovers all around. The Great Death? Here, soon, the time arrives again – of his dominion, in its here-and-now incarnation . . . 'I said, but I did not say with fire and not with Abach [the term for Atomic Biological Chemical warfare]' . . . And the rainbow in the cloud – even it is not visible in the dark of Sabbath eve, on a summery day in autumn.

# Appendix
## Ghetto in an Annihilation Camp:
## Jewish Social History in the Holocaust
## Period and its Ultimate Limits[1]

### I

This article deals with a unique case, which, in addition to its significance as a subject in its own right, provides us with opportunities
to examine a number of fundamental problems of Jewish history in
the Holocaust period regarding an all but incomparable situation of
human and social existence in extremis. The following is a summary
of the salient facts in the history of the 'family camp' at Auschwitz.
The camp was established in September 1943 with the arrival of
5,000 Jews who had been deported from Theresienstadt. Contrary to
the standard procedure at Auschwitz, they did not undergo the selection process, followed by the liquidation of those declared 'unfit for
labour', but were placed in a separate camp at Auschwitz II-Birkenau,
where – again in contrast to routine practice at the other Auschwitz
camps – the men, women and children were allowed to remain within
a single camp and were distinguished from the rest of the prisoners by
their clothes and the fact that their heads were not shaven. Except for
the position of the 'Camp Elder' (*Lagerälteste*), which was filled by a
veteran German criminal inmate of Auschwitz, the internal administration of the camp was left in the hands of the Jews. Nevertheless, the
harsh living conditions in the camp engendered an extremely high
rate of 'natural deaths' (more than 1,000 out of the 5,000 people
brought in the first transport succumbed during the first six months).
Three months later, in December 1943, another transport arrived from
Theresienstadt carrying an additional 5,000 Jews, who were granted
the same conditions and placed in the same camp.

The reason for the special status of these deportees was clear neither to the Jews in the family camp nor to the inmates of the other camps in Auschwitz, but everyone assumed that, for whatever reason, they were exempt from the ordeal imposed on all the other Jews deported to Auschwitz. On 7 March 1944, however, six months after the arrival of the first transport, all those who had come to the camp in September 1943 were annihilated in the gas chambers in a single night without first being subject to the selection procedure applied to the inmates of the other camps in Auschwitz. A few days before their execution, they were ordered to send postcards to the Theresienstadt ghetto and acquaintances in the Third Reich and neutral countries. These postcards bore the date 25 March, that is, more than two weeks after the date on which the members of the first transport were murdered. Meanwhile, those who had arrived in the second transport continued to retain their special status, and in May they were joined by another two transports of 5,000 Jews each from Theresienstadt. But from March onward it was clear to all involved that the lifespan of each transport brought to the special camp was predetermined at precisely six months. Indeed, in July 1944, six months after the arrival of the second transport, another liquidation operation was carried out. This one differed from the first, however, in two ways: (1) The selection procedure was applied, and those declared 'fit for labour' were sent to labour camps in Germany; and (2) all of the rest of the camp was liquidated in one stroke.

Various theories have been advanced to explain the phenomenon of this special camp, but until recently it has not been possible to substantiate them on the basis of any official document. Now, however, with the discovery of a series of documents of the Reich Security Main Office (RSHA) that deal with this subject, we are able to determine the reasons behind the establishment of the camp and the circumstances leading to its liquidation.

Among the relevant documents is an exchange of letters between the Berlin office of the German Red Cross and Eichmann's office in the RSHA, on the one hand, and the International Red Cross headquarters in Geneva, on the other. An examination of these letters leads to the almost certain conclusion that similar and in addition to the Theresienstadt ghetto, this special family camp at Auschwitz was

designed to serve as allegedly living proof that reports about the annihilation of the Jews deported to the East were false. The evidence to
refute those reports included postcards from Auschwitz confirming
that the deportees and their families were alive; the receipt of packages sent through the auspices of the International Red Cross; and the
projected visit to the camp by a Red Cross delegation as a corollary
of a visit to the Theresienstadt ghetto. It appears, however, that the
extremely positive report of the Red Cross commission that visited
the Theresienstadt ghetto (which, in the words of one of the authors
of the RSHA letters, 'satisfied all their expectations') rendered the
second part of the proposed visit – to 'a Jewish labour camp in Birkenau' – superfluous. Thus the final liquidation of the special camp –
which had also become superfluous – was executed shortly after the
Red Cross delegation visited the Theresienstadt ghetto.

## II

As noted at the opening of this article, the case of the 'family camp' in
Auschwitz-Birkenau enables us to examine a number of basic problems of Jewish history in the Holocaust period. I am referring first and
foremost to the issue of the perpetuation of Jewish society as a social
organism under the conditions imposed by the totalitarian regime of
the Third Reich, or to be more precise, the question of the continuity
and limits of Jewish communal life from 1933 up to and throughout
the phase of the mass deportations and annihilation process.

As a result of the findings of recent research into Jewish society
under the rule of the Third Reich, we are able to state that together
with partial manifestations of paralysis and internal disintegration,
the dominant trend evidenced from 1933 onward was a surprising
intensification of various types of internal activity and the perpetuation of various social and spiritual factions. Especially prominent is
the enhanced importance of the community's existing organizational
frameworks and the creation of new structures to deal with education, culture, employment, welfare and the like. This trend continues
to be evident in Germany up to the stage of the mass deportations in
1941–3 and even while these deportations were going on.

It can likewise be distinguished among the deportees to the Theresienstadt ghetto, which absorbed a substantial portion of Germany's remaining Jews. At the same time, with the expansion of the Third Reich and the concentration of Jews in ghettos, similar trends can be discerned in other countries, and it appears that alongside signs of social disintegration and corruption in the ghettos, Jewish society was further consolidated under these severe conditions in somewhat of an accelerated extension of this trend.

On the other hand, when dealing with the existence of Jews in the concentration camps, it appears that we cannot apply this standard of 'continuity', for here the communal frameworks underwent a process of atomization. I am speaking particularly of the existence of those Jews who remained in the camps after the deportations from the ghettos and the liquidation of the 'unfit for labour', including most of the family members of those last survivors. This situation may perhaps allow us to speak of a continuation of the history of Jews qua individuals, but no longer of the continuity of Jewish history, in the sense defined at the beginning of this section.

The 'family camp' of Jews from Theresienstadt in the heart of the Auschwitz-Birkenau annihilation camp, complete with its own leadership and intensive communal activities, provides us with an opportunity to delve into two parallel dimensions of Jewish existence during the Holocaust period: the perpetuity of *the Jews as a society* even in face of the mass-extermination process, alongside the survival of *Jews as individuals* within the multinational prisoner population of the Nazis' largest concentration and annihilation camp.

Among the other issues that may be elucidated by an examination of this subject – but which are not necessarily developed in the discussion below – we should note the following:

1. The efforts of the SS to camouflage the annihilation of the Jews deported to the East – especially in the wake of rising public concern in the free world over this issue – and the equivocal role of the International Red Cross in this stratagem.

2. The efforts of the Jews in the annihilation camps to warn the inhabitants of the ghettos of the fate of the deportees and to arouse world public opinion (*inter alia* by escaping from the camp to return

to the Theresienstadt ghetto and by passing information about Auschwitz on to neutral countries).

3. The ways in which the Jewish leaders and members of the community coped with the prospect of their inevitable liquidation (including the option of resistance, contacts with the camp underground and the *Sonderkommando* crematoria workers, and expressions of collective and individual defiance by the inmates as they knowingly went to their death).

4. The impact of the way of life and liquidation of the inmates of the 'family camp' on their surroundings in Auschwitz – meaning Jews and non-Jews alike – and even on the SS, as manifested in the sources.

In this framework, we are naturally unable to enter into all these problems at length and will have to content ourselves with noting the opportunity to study them on the basis of the sources at our disposal.

## III

Let us now return to the central question of our discussion. Throughout the existence of this special camp, its inhabitants administered their lives in several spheres as a continuation of the communal life and activities they had pursued in Theresienstadt. At the centre of life in the camp was the educational programme, which in turn gave rise to an intensive cultural life. As noted above, in contrast to the rule in the rest of the camps of Auschwitz, the internal administrative functions in the 'family camp', such as block leaders (*Blockälteste*), Kapos and the leaders of labour units, were filled by the Jews themselves. Most of these functionaries were veteran inmates of the Theresienstadt ghetto and some of them came from the ghetto's leadership echelon. However, the foremost authority in the camp, in the estimation of both the inmates and the SS, though not in any formal sense, was the head of the education and youth centre, Fredy Hirsch.

Until the liquidation of the members of the first transport from Theresienstadt everyone believed that the special status of the 'family camp' protected them from being sent to the gas chambers, which operated only a few hundred yards away and in which hundreds of thousands of Jews brought to Auschwitz from all over Europe and thousands of prisoners singled out in the selections as 'unfit for labour' were liquidated during that period. Following the total liquidation of the first transport at the end of its allocated six months, the remaining inmates of the special camp apparently continued to run their lives according to the established patterns of activity: the medical staff continued to make every effort to save the lives of the sick and the elderly; educational and youth activities went on as before; and concerts and theatrical performances continued to be held. Even ideological disputes continued among the various social and religious factions about everything from their competing visions of the ideal future for mankind to the most desirable form of Jewish settlement in Palestine. In contrast to the earlier period, however, all these activities now took place despite the full awareness that all the camp's inmates were doomed to extinction on predetermined dates. Not even those who would otherwise be classified as 'fit for labour' had any chance to evade the common fate – a hope that remained to the rest of the inmates of Auschwitz.

One issue that clearly occupied everyone's thoughts was the way in which they would face their deaths, especially in light of reports about how the members of the first transport had conducted themselves at the end: the last-minute suicide of Fredy Hirsch, attempts at resistance by a number of other leading functionaries, and the singing of *Hatikvah*, the anthem of the Jewish state-in-the-making, the Czech national anthem, and the Internationale, from the depths of the subterranean gas chambers (or, as Gradowski put it in his diary – discovered buried in Auschwitz – 'singing from within the grave').

If I may be allowed to comment here, this act was a kind of 'confession of faith' of the three secular movements of political messianism, with which most of Central European Jewry identified at that time: the Zionist movement; the movement that believed the redemption of the Jews lay in their integration within the national movements of the people among whom they lived; and the socialist movement, with its promise of universal salvation. The traditional Jewish confession of faith, of course, was a matter between man and God. Indirectly, from another source, we actually learn of this manner of confronting what seemed to be an unavoidable fate, from the memoirs of a survivor of the 'family camp', Rabbi Sinai Adler.

Yet another unique message was sent from the threshold of the gas chambers – a powerful, poetic, personal statement by an anonymous twenty-year-old poetess who delivered a stinging indictment in the name of the millions who were consumed by the flames and whose ashes were strewn to the winds. Her ostensibly personal message also speaks to, or on behalf of, 'a generation of slaughtered European youth' sacrificed on the altar of war as they blindly followed the bewitching but fraudulent slogans of their leaders. Her message, however, also demonstrates her abiding commitment to humanism and, indeed, to the radical moral ideal of an utter rejection, whatever the cost may be, of all violence and bloodshed.

It seems that throughout its history, this special camp at Auschwitz-Birkenau was marked by the extrapolation of a situation generally familiar to us from the earlier stages of the Jewish experience within the Third Reich, namely, the tendency to continue fostering communal life and prevent the disintegration of Jewish society as a way of coping with and adjusting to the new conditions, severe though they may have seemed. The radical difference is that in every other situation, including that of the ghettos during the periods of mass deportations, the prospect of future existence essentially remained an open question, while in the case of the 'family camp', the society and its structures including the educational programme, which by its very nature was designed to inculcate values and prepare for the future – continued to function in a situation in which the one incontestable certainty was that of impending death. (This certainty applied not merely in the individual sense but even more so in the sense of a death sentence on the entire community of the special camp as part and parcel of the common destiny of genocide which they themselves witnessed being perpetrated against the Jewish people.)

This remarkable phenomenon of sustaining the structures, activities and values of Jewish society (whose genuine purpose was to safeguard the perpetuation of Jewish life) in a situation that categorically denied any point to purposeful existence can be understood in several ways. One that I believe to be worthy of special consideration is that here, historical, functional and normative values and patterns of life were transformed into something on the order of absolute values.

IV

I now wish to turn briefly to what may be called the 'political history' of the camp and the official documents that shed light on one of the crudest and most cynical attempts to mislead world public opinion regarding the mass extermination of the Jews by exploiting an international humanitarian organization. The architect and orchestrator of this plan was most probably Adolf Eichmann. The documents originate from Eichmann's department in the RSHA, the German Red Cross in Berlin and the International Red Cross in Geneva. They have been found in two unclassified packages of papers in the American 'Document Center' in West Berlin.

The first piece of evidence is from 4 March 1943, about half a year before the establishment of the 'family camp'. It is an important letter from the representative of the German Red Cross in Berlin to the International Red Cross in Geneva relating to the dispatch of food and drugs to the Theresienstadt ghetto. The section relevant to our discussion states:

Further on you asked me about the possibility of sending parcels to Jews in camps in the East. Herewith I must inform you that for practical reasons no such dispatches are possible for the time being. In the event that such a possibility arises in the future, the German Red Cross will return to dealing with this matter.

The next citation comes from a letter sent by the same representative about a year later, on 14 March 1944 – that is, about half a year after the establishment of the 'family camp' in Birkenau. The letter is addressed to the RSHA and is based upon a conversation with Eichmann held shortly before the liquidation of the members of the first transport to the 'family camp'. Here the subject is not merely the packages sent from Switzerland to Theresienstadt and the Jewish camp in Birkenau but the possibility of a visit to these two places:

Referring to the discussion between the undersigned and *Sturmbann-führer* Günther of the 6th of this month and earlier conversation with *Obersturmbannführer* Eichmann regarding the possibility of a visit by a representative of the International Red Cross Committee accredited in Germany to the Old Age Ghetto Theresienstadt, we are now request-ing that a date for this visit be set. [. . .] At the same time, we should like to refer to the previously discussed plan to visit a Jewish labour or penal camp. [. . .] During this visit, it would be appropriate to distribute the parcels of food and medical supplies to the ailing in accordance with your permit 4a, 4b of January 26 [. . .] so that it will be possible to confirm to the United Relief Organization in Geneva receipt of the parcels on the basis of the eyewitness testimony of a representative of the German Red Cross. [. . .] Considering the rise in the number of foreign inquiries about the various Jewish camps, these planned visits to the camps seem to be highly advisable.

Indeed, a further letter, dated 18 May 1944, grants permission for a delegation from the International Red Cross to visit the camp, with early June cited as a desirable date. The letter is from the RSHA to the Director of Foreign Relations of the German Red Cross, Niehaus, and it states, *inter alia*:

The *Reichsführer SS* [Himmler] consented to conduct a tour of inspec-tion of the Theresienstadt ghetto and one Jewish labour camp [in Birkenau] to be undertaken by you and a representative of the Inter-national Red Cross delegation. [. . .]

The words 'one Jewish labour camp' and 'a representative of the International Red Cross delegation' are underlined by hand, and a note was scrawled to the left: 'Transmitted by phone to the Swiss dele-gation on May 19 at 18.00 in the afternoon,' to Dr Marti. The letter regarding this matter, sent to Geneva the next day, has also been preserved.

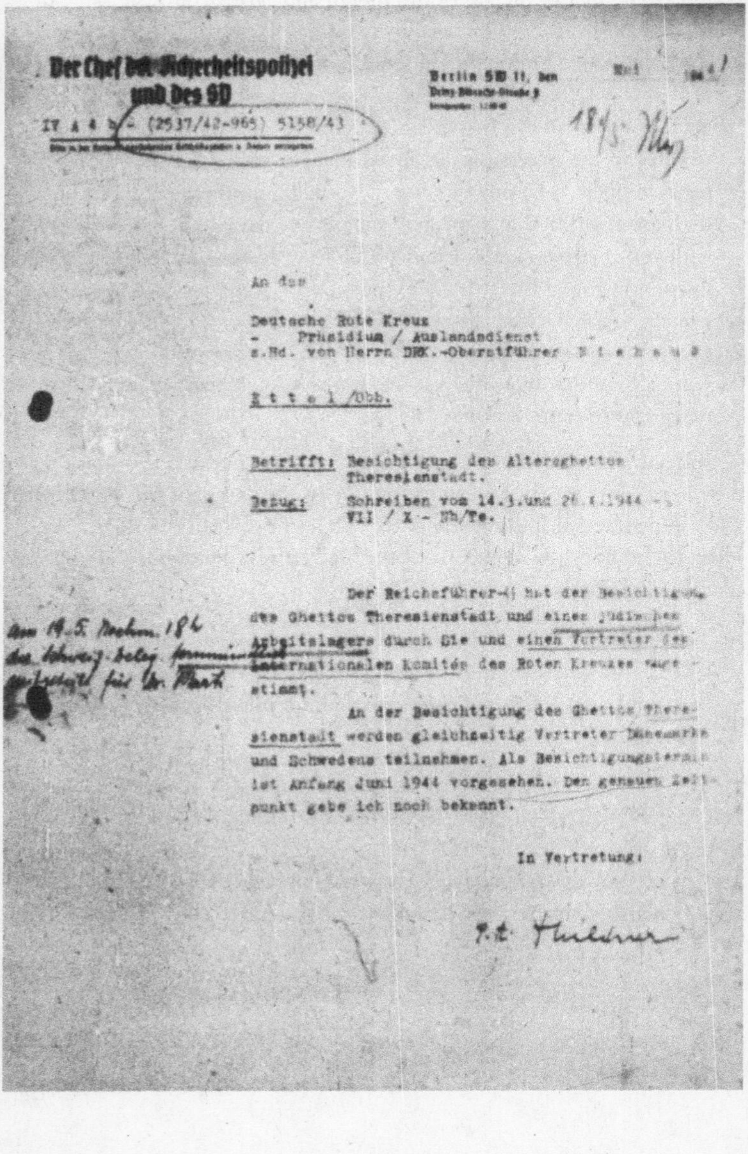

Many documents report about the first part of the visit to the Theresienstadt ghetto on 23 June 1944. As an example, we will cite a section from a letter written by a German Red Cross participant in the tour, Heydekampf, to his superior in Berlin, Niehaus:

> As already reported by phone on Sunday, the undersigned saw the report of [the International Red Cross representative] Dr Rössel. The undersigned has personally reported: to *Hauptsturmführer* Möhs of the RSHA, who seems to have received [the report] with unqualified satisfaction. The matter thus appears to be settled.

A perusal of the attached selections from the International Red Cross report reveals the main reason for the RSHA representative's 'unqualified satisfaction'. For together with the enthusiastic description of the arrangements in the ghetto, it includes the statement that: 'Theresienstadt was portrayed to the members of the delegation as a final camp.' Thus the members of the International Red Cross were explicitly told that there were no further deportations from Theresienstadt to the East. And since, contrary to expectations, the delegation did not raise any further questions, it was clear that the visit to Theresienstadt satisfied all their desires.

Thus the answer prepared to satisfy all possible questions regarding the fate of those deported to the East, namely, the 'family camp' in Auschwitz-Birkenau, became superfluous. And so, less than three weeks after this visit, during the first half of July, the camp was finally liquidated.

# List of Illustrations

1. Auschwitz-Birkenau, January 1945 (United States Holocaust Memorial Museum, Photo Archives)
2. Auschwitz-Birkenau, summer 1978: ruins of the electric fence between the quarantine camp BIIa and the 'family camp' BIIb (photo: O. D. Kulka)
3. Auschwitz-Birkenau, summer 1978: ruins of the 'family camp' BIIb (photo: O. D. Kulka)
4. Auschwitz-Birkenau: piece of a brick from the ruins of Crematorium No. II, 1978 (photo collection of O. D. Kulka)
5. Auschwitz-Birkenau: ruins of Crematorium No. I (photo: papers of Erich Kulka, collection of O. D. Kulka)
6. Auschwitz-Birkenau: ruins of Crematorium No. I, stairs leading down into the gas chamber (Auschwitz-Birkenau State Museum)
7. Auschwitz-Birkenau, summer 1978: the gate and the tracks leading to the 'ramp' (photo: anonymous taxi driver from Kraków; collection of O. D. Kulka)
8. Front of a postcard from Anna Schmolková from the 'family camp' to Georgine Baum in Prague, sent via the *Reichsvereinigung der Juden in Deutschland*, Berlin, dated 25 March 1944 (Auschwitz-Birkenau Postcards Collection, Jewish Museum in Prague)
9. Back of the postcard (see no. 8).
10. Marianná Langová, born 27.2.1932, died in Auschwitz 6.10.1944 (Terezin's Children Drawings Collection, Jewish Museum in Prague)
11. Anna Klausnerová, born 23.07.1932, died in Auschwitz 12.10.1944 (Terezin's Children Drawings Collection, Jewish Museum in Prague)

# Notes

## INTRODUCTION

1. *Deutsches Judentum unter dem Nationalsozialismus,* Tübingen 1997; *Die Juden in den geheimen NS-Stimmungsberichten 1933–1945,* hrsg. zus. mit Eberhard Jäckel, Düsseldorf 2004; Engl. ed.: *The Jews in the Secret Nazi Reports on Popular Opinion in Germany 1933–1945,* New Haven, Conn., 2010.

2. On the history of the camp, see my article based on the available documentary material on this special camp, reprinted in the appendix to the present book.

## CHAPTER 1. A PROLOGUE THAT COULD ALSO BE AN EPILOGUE

1. 'The Churches in the Third Reich and the "Jewish Question" in the Light of the Secret Nazi Reports on German "Public Opinion"' (Congrès de Varsovie, 25 Juin–1er Juillet 1978, section IV: Les Églises chrétiennes dans l'Europe dominée par le IIIe Reich), *Bibliothèque de la Revue d'Histoire Ecclésiastique,* 70 (1984), pp. 490–505.

## CHAPTER 2. BETWEEN THERESIENSTADT AND AUSCHWITZ

1. *The Selected Poetry of Dan Pagis,* trans. Stephen Mitchell (Berkeley, 1989), p. 29.

2. See Appendix.

3. A term used in Zionist youth movements for which no exact translation exists; from the Hebrew root for 'way' or 'path', hence a guide, instructor

and informal educator rolled into one; plural: *madrichim* (*Translator's note*).

4. Imre was his nickname in the youth block; his real name was Emmerich Acs. He was born 28.09.1912, deported to Auschwitz from Theresienstadt on 06.09.1943 and died in the gas chamber on 08.03.1944. See Miroslav Kárný *et al.* (eds.), *Terezínská pamětní kniha: Židovské oběti nacistických deportací z Čech a Moravy* (The Theresienstadt Memorial Book: Jewish Victims of the Nazi Deportations from Bohemia and Moravia) (Prague, 1995), vol. 2, p. 1209.

## CHAPTER 5. OBSERVATIONS AND PERPLEXITIES ABOUT SCENES IN THE MEMORY

1. http://www.yadvashem.org/odot_pdf/Microsoft%20Word%20-%202489.pdf

## CHAPTER 8. LANDSCAPES OF A PRIVATE MYTHOLOGY

1. The Gate of Mercy, known also as the Golden Gate, is one of the major portals in the Old City wall. Built in the Byzantine period, it was sealed from both the inside and the outside during the construction of the Ottoman wall in the sixteenth century. According to Jewish and Christian legends, it is through this gate that the Messiah will enter Jerusalem.

2. According to Muslim legend, the Jewish Messiah who will enter Jerusalem through this gate is from the priestly family (*Kohanim*) and hence will be prevented from entering by the presence of graves, which cause ritual impurity. It is for this reason, the legend says, that a Muslim cemetery – which continues to function to this day – was established outside the gate.

## CHAPTER 11. DREAM: JEWISH PRAGUE AND THE GREAT DEATH

1. In 1942 the Nazi regime established in Prague the Central Jewish Museum, with the goal of preserving a memory of an exterminated race, by collecting notable objects of Jewish ceremonial art from the

liquidated Jewish communities of Bohemia and Moravia. This had to be done by the last still remaining Jews in Prague at that time. See Hana Volavková, *A Story of the Jewish Museum in Prague* (Prague, 1968).

## CHAPTER 13. GOD'S GRIEVING

1. During the waiting period for the second Gulf War, in expectation of a gas and nuclear attack on Israel (October 2002–March 2003).
2. 'I have placed My rainbow in the clouds, and it shall be a sign of the covenant between Me and the earth. There will never again be a flood to destroy the earth' (Genesis 9: 11–13).
3. 'You vowed that You would not bring a flood, and now, if You do not bring a flood of water into the world but a flood of fire and brimstone, You will not be keeping Your vow. And if You renege on the vow, heaven forbid.' From *Midrash Sechel Tov*, by Menachem Ben Salomo, an Italian (or Provençal) rabbi of the twelfth century; published by Salomon Buber (of Lvov) (Berlin, 1900); on Genesis 18, the destruction of Sodom and Gomorrah.
4. Ecclesiastes 1: 9.
5. The origin of the Hebrew phrase *haba aleinu letova* stems from Jewish liturgical language. It means 'may it be for our good' or 'may it be for a blessing on us'. In the context of this text, it may express a sense of sarcasm and resignation (*Translator's note*).
6. Job 2: 10.
7. Transcription of the dream image I recorded in the diary that was lost. The entry was made shortly after the fearful days and weeks of expectation here in May 1967 of a war that would be launched from all directions. It was also incorporated at the time in a letter to my father, in Prague – cryptic, implicit and concrete – in a drawing of the 'map of the imprints of the Great Death' as a shiny black aerial photograph, with only the lethal radiation pervading everything, as a 'sign of life'. Perhaps this was the very letter that my father took with him before he escaped in that storm when the tanks thundered through the streets of Prague. Could it now be among his papers in the Yad Vashem Archives?
8. Diary entry, 22 January 2001, ch. 12 above.
9. Based on the notes I made on the day after the dream, on 12 August 2002.
10. In Dan Pagis's letter from his sabbatical in San Diego to me in Jerusalem, 28 January 1976: 'The subject-matter in Gerschon's poems is

painfully difficult for me: it is a subject I fled from for twenty-five years and more. Not until a few years ago did it overtake me (vanquish me, if you will) in my writing. Nevertheless, I was caught up in Gerschon's poems and at one time I tried to translate two or three of them – I have been familiar with all the ones you sent me for some time. I tried, and I despaired. I cannot convey the allusion to bone marrow in *Mark* within *des . . . Markgrafen Gomorras*. No duke, earl, Margrave and so forth is understood *from the outset* by the Hebrew reader to the point where this reader can grasp its *metamorphosis* in the poem.' Indeed, this poem was not included in the bilingual German–Hebrew selection of Gerschon's poetry (see following note) and remains part of his literary estate, of which I am the executor.

11. Gerschon: 'und ich fragte / bin ich der Hüter meines Bruders / KAIN' ('and I asked / am I my brother / CAIN's keeper; Gerschon Ben-David, *In den Wind Werfen: Versuche um Metabarbarisches. Gedichte*, Straelener Manuskripte (Straelen, 1995), pp. 12–13. Cf. Genesis 4: 9). Dan's poem reads:

### Autobiography

I died with the first blow and was buried
among the rocks of the field.
The raven taught my parents
what to do with me.

If my family is famous,
not a little of the credit goes to me.
My brother invented murder,
my parents invented grief,
I invented silence.

Afterwards the well-known events took place.
Our inventions were perfected. One thing led to another,
orders were given. There were those who murdered in their
    own way,
grieved in their own way.

I won't mention names
out of consideration for the reader,
since at first the details horrify
though finally they're a bore:

you can die once, twice, even seven times,
but you can't die a thousand times.
I can.
My underground cells reach everywhere.

When Cain began to multiply on the face of the earth,
I began to multiply in the belly of the earth,
and my strength has long been greater than his.
His legions desert him and go over to me,
and even this is only half a revenge.

*The Selected Poetry of Dan Pagis*, trans. Stephen Mitchell (Berkeley, 1989), pp. 5–6.

12. What I say here runs counter to Resh Lakish's assertion, 'Job never existed and was just a parable' (Babylonian Talmud, I 15a); and counter to Maimonides in *Guide for the Perplexed* (part III, c. 22); but resonates with Dan Pagis's grieving 'Homily': 'From the start, the forces were unequal: Satan a grand seigneur in heaven, Job mere flesh and blood. And anyway, the contest was unfair. Job, who had lost all his wealth and had been bereaved of his sons and daughters and stricken with loathsome boils, wasn't even aware that it was a contest. Because he complained too much, the referee silenced him. So, having accepted this decision, in silence, he defeated his opponent without even realizing it. Therefore his wealth was restored, he was given sons and daughters – new ones, of course – and his grief for the first children was taken away. We might imagine that this retribution was the most terrible thing of all. We might imagine that the most terrible thing was Job's ignorance: not understanding whom he had defeated, or even that he had won. *But in fact, the most terrible thing of all is that Job never existed and was just a parable* [my italics]', ibid., p. 11.

13. Job 2: 7.

# APPENDIX

1. First published in Yisrael Gutman and Avital Saf (eds.), *The Nazi Concentration Camps: Structure and Aims, the Image of the Prisoner, the Jews in the Camps* (Jerusalem, 1984), pp. 315–33. The published version, with a detailed scholarly apparatus omitted here, is accessible on the internet: http://lekket.com/data/articles/004-000-018_000.pdf.

ALLEN LANE
*an imprint of*
PENGUIN BOOKS

# Also Published

Martyn Rady, *The Habsburgs: The Rise and Fall of a World Power*

John Gooch, *Mussolini's War: Fascist Italy from Triumph to Collapse, 1935-1943*

Roger Scruton, *Wagner's Parsifal: The Music of Redemption*

Roberto Calasso, *The Celestial Hunter*

Benjamin R. Teitelbaum, *War for Eternity: The Return of Traditionalism and the Rise of the Populist Right*

Laurence C. Smith, *Rivers of Power: How a Natural Force Raised Kingdoms, Destroyed Civilizations, and Shapes Our World*

Sharon Moalem, *The Better Half: On the Genetic Superiority of Women*

Augustine Sedgwick, *Coffeeland: A History*

Daniel Todman, *Britain's War: A New World, 1942-1947*

Anatol Lieven, *Climate Change and the Nation State: The Realist Case*

Blake Gopnik, *Warhol: A Life as Art*

Malena and Beata Ernman, Svante and Greta Thunberg, *Our House is on Fire: Scenes of a Family and a Planet in Crisis*

Paolo Zellini, *The Mathematics of the Gods and the Algorithms of Men: A Cultural History*

Bari Weiss, *How to Fight Anti-Semitism*

Lucy Jones, *Losing Eden: Why Our Minds Need the Wild*

Brian Greene, *Until the End of Time: Mind, Matter, and Our Search for Meaning in an Evolving Universe*

Anastasia Nesvetailova and Ronen Palan, *Sabotage: The Business of Finance*

Albert Costa, *The Bilingual Brain: And What It Tells Us about the Science of Language*

Stanislas Dehaene, *How We Learn: The New Science of Education and the Brain*

Daniel Susskind, *A World Without Work: Technology, Automation and How We Should Respond*

John Tierney and Roy F. Baumeister, *The Power of Bad: And How to Overcome It*

Greta Thunberg, *No One Is Too Small to Make a Difference: Illustrated Edition*

Glenn Simpson and Peter Fritsch, *Crime in Progress: The Secret History of the Trump-Russia Investigation*

Abhijit V. Banerjee and Esther Duflo, *Good Economics for Hard Times: Better Answers to Our Biggest Problems*

Gaia Vince, *Transcendence: How Humans Evolved through Fire, Language, Beauty and Time*

Roderick Floud, *An Economic History of the English Garden*

Rana Foroohar, *Don't Be Evil: The Case Against Big Tech*

Ivan Krastev and Stephen Holmes, *The Light that Failed: A Reckoning*

Andrew Roberts, *Leadership in War: Lessons from Those Who Made History*

Alexander Watson, *The Fortress: The Great Siege of Przemysl*

Stuart Russell, *Human Compatible: AI and the Problem of Control*

Serhii Plokhy, *Forgotten Bastards of the Eastern Front: An Untold Story of World War II*

Dominic Sandbrook, *Who Dares Wins: Britain, 1979-1982*

Charles Moore, *Margaret Thatcher: The Authorized Biography, Volume Three: Herself Alone*

Thomas Penn, *The Brothers York: An English Tragedy*

David Abulafia, *The Boundless Sea: A Human History of the Oceans*

Anthony Aguirre, *Cosmological Koans: A Journey to the Heart of Physics*

Orlando Figes, *The Europeans: Three Lives and the Making of a Cosmopolitan Culture*

Naomi Klein, *On Fire: The Burning Case for a Green New Deal*

Anne Boyer, *The Undying: A Meditation on Modern Illness*

Benjamin Moser, *Sontag: Her Life*

Daniel Markovits, *The Meritocracy Trap*

Malcolm Gladwell, *Talking to Strangers: What We Should Know about the People We Don't Know*

Peter Hennessy, *Winds of Change: Britain in the Early Sixties*

John Sellars, *Lessons in Stoicism: What Ancient Philosophers Teach Us about How to Live*

Brendan Simms, *Hitler: Only the World Was Enough*

Hassan Damluji, *The Responsible Globalist: What Citizens of the World Can Learn from Nationalism*

Peter Gatrell, *The Unsettling of Europe: The Great Migration, 1945 to the Present*

Justin Marozzi, *Islamic Empires: Fifteen Cities that Define a Civilization*

Bruce Hood, *Possessed: Why We Want More Than We Need*

Susan Neiman, *Learning from the Germans: Confronting Race and the Memory of Evil*

Donald D. Hoffman, *The Case Against Reality: How Evolution Hid the Truth from Our Eyes*

Frank Close, *Trinity: The Treachery and Pursuit of the Most Dangerous Spy in History*

Richard M. Eaton, *India in the Persianate Age: 1000-1765*

Janet L. Nelson, *King and Emperor: A New Life of Charlemagne*

Philip Mansel, *King of the World: The Life of Louis XIV*

Donald Sassoon, *The Anxious Triumph: A Global History of Capitalism, 1860-1914*

Elliot Ackerman, *Places and Names: On War, Revolution and Returning*

Jonathan Aldred, *Licence to be Bad: How Economics Corrupted Us*

Johny Pitts, *Afropean: Notes from Black Europe*

Walt Odets, *Out of the Shadows: Reimagining Gay Men's Lives*

James Lovelock, *Novacene: The Coming Age of Hyperintelligence*

Mark B. Smith, *The Russia Anxiety: And How History Can Resolve It*

Stella Tillyard, *George IV: King in Waiting*

Jonathan Rée, *Witcraft: The Invention of Philosophy in English*

Jared Diamond, *Upheaval: How Nations Cope with Crisis and Change*

Emma Dabiri, *Don't Touch My Hair*

Srecko Horvat, *Poetry from the Future: Why a Global Liberation Movement Is Our Civilisation's Last Chance*

Paul Mason, *Clear Bright Future: A Radical Defence of the Human Being*

Remo H. Largo, *The Right Life: Human Individuality and its role in our development, health and happiness*

Joseph Stiglitz, *People, Power and Profits: Progressive Capitalism for an Age of Discontent*

David Brooks, *The Second Mountain*

Roberto Calasso, *The Unnamable Present*

Lee Smolin, *Einstein's Unfinished Revolution: The Search for What Lies Beyond the Quantum*

Clare Carlisle, *Philosopher of the Heart: The Restless Life of Søren Kierkegaard*

Nicci Gerrard, *What Dementia Teaches Us About Love*

Edward O. Wilson, *Genesis: On the Deep Origin of Societies*

John Barton, *A History of the Bible: The Book and its Faiths*

Carolyn Forché, *What You Have Heard is True: A Memoir of Witness and Resistance*

Elizabeth-Jane Burnett, *The Grassling*

Kate Brown, *Manual for Survival: A Chernobyl Guide to the Future*